AF325839

Governing by Chaos
Social engineering and globalization

Lucien Cerise

GOVERNING BY CHAOS
Social engineering and globalization

Max Milo

ESSAIS - DOCUMENTS

Max Milo, Paris, 2023
www.maxmilo.com
ISBN : 9782315011964

*"When the government violates the rights of the people,
insurrection is, for the people and for every portion of the people,
the most sacred of rights and the most indispensable of duties."*

Declaration of the Rights of Man and the Citizen,
1793, article 35.

Introduction
Social engineering,
or cunning in the service of utopia

In recent years, the term social engineering has gained currency in describing phenomena of accelerated social change such as those that occurred during the coronavirus crisis. One possible definition of social engineering is the methodical and stealthy transformation of social subjects, individuals or groups. In their book on the Great *Reset*, published in 2020, Klaus Schwab, president of the World Economic Forum (Davos Forum), and Thierry Malleret, consultant, describe the concerted deployment on a planetary scale of a new transhumanist reality under the pretext of the Covid-19 epidemic.[1] From the exploitation of a crisis to its orchestration, there is only one step, which some people in power may be tempted to take, as Naomi Klein has shown in her various publications on "disaster capitalism". Social engineering can thus be embodied in the figure of the pyromaniac firefighter, who is not content to take advantage of moments of crisis, but who also knows how to provoke them in order to advance his agenda. Or how to provide solutions to problems that you have created yourself. This intuitive approach was refined in the 20th century in the two methodological sets that underpin the theory

---

1. SCHWAB (Klaus), MALLERET (Thierry), *COVID-19: the Great Reset*, Forum Publishing, 2020.

and practice of social engineering: on the one hand, group management and, on the other, information security - defense and attack, espionage and hacking.

The founding father of management is the American Frederik Taylor (1856-1915), who laid the foundations of the scientific organization of work (SOW). Social engineering, or the scientific organization of society, is a managerial approach to the social fact of "change management". This method, theorized by John Kotter, professor of management at Harvard, consists of eight steps, the first of which consists of creating a sense of urgency in the target population in order to destabilize it and engage it in a process aimed at making it change. The objective reality of the urgency, as well as its real origin, are secondary issues here. The success of this first step makes it possible to gradually start moving the "Overton window", i.e. the window of tolerance of new habits - and new *habitus* - that the target group can support, adopt and finally normalize. This process makes it possible to gradually and discreetly modify the state of society without asking for the informed consent of the individuals who compose it, or by manufacturing their consent, *"Engineering of Consent"*, according to Edward Bernays' formula. Beyond mass manipulation, whose impact is punctual, social engineering has a definitive aim. The sciences of behavior and the influence of behavior are put at the service of a project of structural reorganization of society, which often involves its controlled demolition in order to rebuild it according to a new plan. Just like certain related disciplines such as building engineering, genetic engineering, computer engineering or financial engineering, social engineering is not content with a theoretical description of its object, in this case social subjects, it also proposes practical recipes for acting on them in order to definitively modify their nature, their identity, as well as the form of the social link. Here lies the great difference between the social sciences, which are purely descriptive, and social engineering, which is not only prescriptive, but also interventionist. In this sense, it has a lot to do with "politics", this voluntarist vision of life in society, which does not stop at looking at what is happening, but which seeks to act materially and durably, and as close as possible to the facts. Politics, in the classical sense of the term, is however an art of persuasion, which addresses the conscious self, the free will, while social engineering aims rather at the unconscious and the subliminal, in a purely technical perspective of hacking minds and subverting behaviors. Within the limits of this introduction, we will present to our readers the history of social engineering by backing it up with two great concepts of political philosophy: utopia and cunning.

The main thread of utopian thought is the notion of ideal in politics - thus of ideal society. The immanent reality, always imperfect, is compared to a transcendent ideal of perfection, that is to say, at a distance, and that one must reach, either by joining it in the afterlife after death, or by realizing it on Earth. This dialectic of utopia and reality is staged by Saint Augustine in his major work, *The City of God*, written between 416 and 423, in which he contrasts the ideal celestial city with the corrupted earthly city. By definition, the heavenly city, whose characteristics evoke paradise, is not of this world. Although it is a source of inspiration for men, the ideal society belongs in the Augustinian thought to the metaphysical register. On their side, the materialistic utopias, which aim at an earthly realization of the ideal, present various aspects more or less mixed, even contradictory. They can be nostalgic and conservative when the model of society belongs to a bygone past that should be re-established - hence the cultural myths of the good savage and of the Edenic golden age of the organic and classless society preceding the fall, the corruption, the commodity, etc. -, but they can also contain elements of nostalgia and conservatism. -but they can also contain revolutionary and progressive elements, when this past or never-existing ideal model is projected into a radiant future to be built. The quest for an ideal always maintains the hope of a "*tabula rasa*" on the existing, either that we wait for the end of times, and therefore the end of the world, so that another world comes to be, or that we decide to accelerate History to make "a clean sweep of the past" and realize the New World here below. This hope of a great beginning is called today by the transhumanists the Great *Reset*. In this eschatological perspective of a temporality oriented by a project to be realized, the metaphysical utopian narratives rely on faith in God's plan, while the materialists turn to human reason and support the idea that it would be possible to scientifically organize society, according to a quasi-geometric plan designed to function more harmoniously.

In the West, the first great materialist utopian text is Plato's *Republic*, written around -315. The second great text that immediately comes to mind is Thomas More's *Utopia*, published in 1516 and which launched the common use of the term utopia, meaning "in no place". The Renaissance is an important milestone in utopian thinking, but it is in the wake of socialism in the nineteenth century that the first concrete realizations appear, with the phalansteres of Charles Fourier and various projects of community life inspired by the positivism of Saint-Simon and Auguste Comte. The mathematician and sociologist Adolphe Quetelet (1796-1874) created the concept of "social physics" around 1830, and then it was the polytechnician and mining engineer Frédéric Le Play (1806-1882) who sought to found a school for social engineers. In this anthropology common to socialism and liberalism, the human being and the world are fundamentally rational, which contrasts with the mysteries of faith. But in all cases, perfection is accessible, either by reaching it in another world, or by achieving it on Earth, and the spirit is in search of the "fusional group", it seeks to put an end once and for all to evil, problems and suffering.

This utopian tradition is opposed to the pragmatic and realist tradition in politics which, as its name indicates, is based primarily on concrete practice and measures the value of its action by its relative effectiveness, without relating it to an absolutist ideal, but by comparing situations that are always contextual. In Friedrich Nietzsche's Great Superhuman Politics, there is no clean slate on Evil, one accepts its presence, there is only an eternal restart, an Eternal Return of Good as well as Evil. We owe it to the epistemologist Karl Popper to have theorized in his works of the 1950s, notably *The Open Society and its Enemies*, the difference between utopian social engineering and pragmatic social engineering, devoid of a systematic aim and proceeding in a fragmented manner. In the same years, the apartheid regime of South Africa decided to apply social engineering in a concrete way to organize racial segregation between whites and blacks throughout the country, with the declared intention of pacifying identity-based tensions, which ended up exactly the opposite of the desired goal. The transhumanist utopia being implemented at an accelerated pace since 2020 also has catastrophic consequences and also provokes reactions of rejection among many people. It is precisely to overcome the natural reticence coming from the instinct of conservation that social engineering has acquired an additional conceptual and methodological tool: the ruse.

A name comes immediately to mind when one evokes cunning in politics: Nicolas Machiavelli, eminent representative of the realist movement and theorist of "extraordinary means". In fact, cunning is as old as the world, it is already found in the animal kingdom, when the predator advances, hidden in the tall grass, to avoid being seen by its prey. A popular French expression speaks of acting with "ruses de Sioux", which is synonymous with deception, dissimulation, duplicity, diversion, decoy, camouflage, stratagem, subterfuge and indirect approach. Several mythologies have invented archetypal figures of cunning, notably the Nordic pantheon, with the god Loki, and before that the Greek with the god Proteus, capable of taking all forms, and the goddess Metis. As early as antiquity, a certain number of reflections on these subjects appear at about the same time and in several cultures, revealing a kind of general awareness, a worldwide *Zeitgeist*. Between the 8th and the 5th century B.C., the human mind is ripe for writing down a certain number of philosophical, literary and religious classics that give a central place to cunning. In China, it is *The Art of War*, attributed to Sun-Tzu, a compendium of various military strategies and tactics. In ancient Greece, Homer wrote *The Iliad* and *The Odyssey*, which feature Odysseus, "the man of a thousand tricks", and the famous "Trojan horse", a tool for infiltrating the enemy, which has become an integral part of the vocabulary in computer *hacking* circles. In the Near East, the first books of the Bible are written. In Deuteronomy 20:10 and 20:11, the basics of social engineering, in the sense of mind hacking and stealthy penetration of a target system, are laid out in a "biblical" style, pithy and bright: "10. When you approach a city to attack it, you will offer it peace. 11. If it accepts peace and opens its gates to you, all the people there will be tributary to you and enslaved." The opening/closing dialectic and the impersonation of a peaceful identity to abuse another's trust to make them open their doors and voluntarily lower their defensive guard are at the heart of the practice of human brain hacking. When the target remains suspicious and closed, it can nevertheless be subjugated after having been surrounded and pushed to surrender, as Deuteronomy still recommends in the following verses: "12. If it will not make peace with you and wants to make war with you, then you shall besiege it. 13. And after the Lord your God has delivered it into your hand, you shall put all the males of it to the sword." Organizing a siege of the target to bring it down is an example of an indirect strategy that is less costly than a frontal attack. Transposed to modern times, in the new circles of power that are the tertiary sector and its bureaucracy, the practice of besieging is called cognitive encirclement, similar to psychological harassment, but more subtle, aiming to marginalize and then exclude an adversary from economic and information warfare.

War has always been psychological, cognitive, cultural, semantic, and therefore linguistic, as well as physical and material. The Greeks and Romans invented sophistry, rhetoric, demagogy and persuasion techniques, what was once called propaganda, renamed in the liberal context as "strategic communication", "public relations" and *storytelling*, or how to tell stories to the general public that mobilize their emotions and build their reality. The reflection on the art of oratory and verbal jousting - and especially how to win them at all costs - will have a long posterity. Medieval Christian scholasticism developed casuistry, of which the Jesuits were the masters, and which became synonymous with idle discussions. In the same spirit, Talmudic Judaism gave birth to *pilpoul*, an exercise consisting in defending specious reasoning to the point of absurdity, the important thing being not that it be true or logical, but only plausible, which seems to have become the watchword of the mass media. All cultures and traditions have theorized their own version of political trickery. Islam offers a number of communication strategies that allow proselytizing Muslims to move forward masked, rhetorical techniques generally grouped under the term *taqiya*, the simulation and concealment of intentions permitted by the Qur'an (Sura 3:28) in dealing with infidels (*kufar*), but also between Shi'a and Sunni Muslims.

More subtle and therefore less detectable than lying, the art of deceiving without lying could be divided into two main trends. The first one consists in playing with double meanings, undertones, connotations and subliminal messages that pass in filigree, which is similar to steganography, or how to hide a message in another message. The second one is called nowadays "perception management", that is to say the lie by omission set up as a method to create a biased reality consisting in highlighting what suits me and ignoring what is not. Talking about the glass being half full - and deliberately forgetting the half empty - or, conversely, only talking about the trains that arrive late and never about those that arrive on time. These communication techniques, known for centuries by traditional cultures, find concrete political applications in our time in image and reputation management, especially during election periods, for example in ways of supporting a candidate without ever campaigning openly for him or her, and even criticizing him or her, but criticizing his or her competitors even more harshly to make him or her appear preferable by contrast. The essential message must be understood in the negative, in what is not said.

From a general point of view, the ruse in politics consists in reversing the Kantian categorical imperative and in considering others as means. This instrumental reductionism in the relationship to others is supported by technoscience and the paradigm of information and communication sciences that emerged after World War II and began to shape the dominant ideology as well as private life. Cybernetics, a discipline invented by Norbert Wiener in the 1940s and 1950s to optimize ballistic calculations, describes the world as a set of interacting systems to be controlled and regulated, and abolishes on the theoretical and practical levels the boundary between subject and object, living and non-living, and therefore human target and moving object. Social engineering, in the sense of computer hacking, consists first of all in *phishing* a human target, i.e. in gaining its trust so that it opens up to me voluntarily and that I can extract information from it or modify its vision of the world with its agreement. The two great references in this field are Kevin Mitnick, who published *The Art of Deception* in 2002, and Christopher Hadnagy, for *Social Engineering: The Art of Human Hacking* in 2010. When another person trusts me, when he opens up to me, he accepts that my code is part of his code, that my word is part of his reality, even that my word becomes his reality, builds his reality, like a small child takes the word of his parents for the absolute truth, or like a hypnotized person takes the subjective word of the hypnotist for the objective reality. The suggestibility of the target is essential and must make it possible to overcome the instinctive distrust and the natural movement of closure animating any living being which seeks to ensure its safety. It is therefore easier to understand why the negative connotation systematically associated with the notion of closure, and the positive connotation just as systematically associated with the notions of openness and open society, comes from this: it is a social engineering and crowd psychology "trick" to better hack and rape them after having mentally disarmed them by making them feel guilty about their natural tendency to close themselves in order to control and filter influences coming from the outside. It is no coincidence that the financier George Soros has given - in homage to his master Karl Popper - the name of Open Society to his network of foundations aiming at breaking down borders and subverting nations and protectionism for the benefit of supranational capital.

To transform the social bond in a group, however, it is not always enough to inspire confidence, one must also know how to increase distrust among others. The psychological operation of the "bleuite" during the Algerian war is a classic of its kind and consisted in spreading the rumor in the Algerian ranks of the FLN (National Liberation Front) and its paramilitary branch the ALN (National Liberation Army) that there were infiltrated agents in the service of the French... when there were none! Captain Paul-Alain Léger, a specialist in psychological warfare, targeted the brain of Colonel Amirouche, leader of Wilaya III in Kabylia, to persuade him through various subterfuges that his sector was infiltrated by spies and double agents working for France. The Algerian *leader* and his organization, convinced of a non-existent problem, began to destroy themselves by launching the purge of those they believed to be traitors in their own camp. Doubt, suspicion, and paranoia spread virally through the ranks of the ALN and FLN for months, leading to bloody purges, without any physical commitment on the part of the French.

Social engineering could more prosaically be called "social subversion". In fact, this approach to social relationships most often consists of dividing to rule, i.e., creating triangulated conflicts by playing on relationships of trust, mistrust and indifference, and by exploiting what transactional analysis calls Karpman's triangle, i.e., the projective system of executioner/victim/savior that weaves the fabric of relationships in all human groups. The projective system is made up of representations that do not necessarily correspond to reality. During the bleeding operation, the belief in the existence of infiltrators that did not exist had the same result as if they had existed: the rise of general distrust, leading to the self-dissolution of the group. Belief in something that does not exist can have the same impact as something that does exist. Fiction can have the same impact on reality as reality itself. One can therefore act on reality from the representation of reality, therefore from language - what traditional cultures call "magic" - and it does not matter whether this representation is true or false. However, one can recognize real infiltrators by the fact that they always try to launch "blueprints" in human groups, that is to say epidemics of paranoia and mutual accusation of belonging to a controlled opposition or to an infiltrated fifth column.

Organizing the powerlessness of the opponent is the first task of power. The agents of division and demoralization work to break the unity of groups, but also the unity of individuals by trying to make them crazy or depressed. Psychological warfare often consists of taking control of the enemy's system of representations in order to push him to do wrong and ultimately to hit himself, which is, once again, less costly than a frontal attack. In this perspective, one must know how to exploit all the resources of what psychology has isolated under the concept of death drive, an expression gathering all the cognitive biases that risk contradicting the instinct of self-preservation. The current of *Dark Psychology* knows how to make an intensive use of it. The notion of *gaslighting*, based on the work of Patrick Hamilton, emerged in the English-speaking world of psychology in the 1950s to describe a sociopathic personality trait that could be used as a method, consisting of manipulating the self-esteem of others by making them feel guilty about what one does oneself through accusatory inversion, a common phenomenon in the victim claims of active minorities and their lobbies. The concept of *"learned helplessness"* invented by Martin Seligman in 1975 was successful with the CIA in order to work on the mechanisms of resignation and how to provoke it in others - in addition to the experiments on human guinea pigs of mental reprogramming, better known under the English term of *mind control.* In the communist world during the Cold War, social engineering was called "political technology" and gave rise to "reflexive control" (Рефлексивное управление), akin to lying poker, a combination of game theory, i.e., the anticipated calculation of the opponent's moves, and *maskirovka* (camouflage), or how to lure the opponent about my intentions in order to send him off on false leads and make him abandon the fight. During the same period, the Stasi in East Germany practiced "decomposition", or *Zersetzung*, which consisted of plunging an individual into permanent uncertainty on all subjects, particularly on his relations of trust with his close relations, in order to push him into delusions of interpretation and persecution, and if possible into depression and suicide.

As one can imagine from these examples, social engineering is inseparable from a panoptic approach to society, in the sense of Michel Foucault, that is to say, reproducing the conditions of a prison-like social control, or even a concentration system. Let's ask ourselves now where we stand in terms of population surveillance. It is clear that things are only getting worse. The progress of technological surveillance and predictive justice, also known as anticipatory or "actuarial" criminology, is ever more invasive and seems to have no limits. At the same time, and in a seemingly paradoxical way, information is also leaking and circulating more and more. The Julian Assange (WikiLeaks) and Edward Snowden (NSA) affairs have had the merit of widely exposing and raising to the highest geopolitical level what had become an open secret, namely that the US spies on the whole world, starting with heads of state and allied countries! But the road to hell is paved with good intentions. Digital dictatorship is progressing in the West under the pretext of ensuring the security of citizens. However, since police surveillance has a bad press in Western societies that are increasingly liberal and libertarian, it has been necessary, in an attempt to manufacture consent to the computer dictatorship, to rely on the representation of a "murderous pandemic" or of a man-made global warming to try to justify the sanitary, vaccinal or climatic pass. In March 2020, the transhumanist Yuval Harari described in an interview with UNESCO the health crisis as an opportunity to facilitate the deployment of surveillance technologies "under the skin": "We are currently witnessing the creation of new surveillance systems around the world, both by states and by companies. The current crisis could mark a major turning point in the history of surveillance. First, it could legitimize and normalize the massive deployment of surveillance tools in countries that have previously rejected them. The second reason is even more important: this crisis could lead to a radical transition from "on-skin" to "under-skin" surveillance. Previously, governments and corporations primarily monitored our actions, tracking where we go and whom we meet. Today, they are more interested in what's going on inside our bodies: our health, our temperature, our blood pressure. This kind of biometric information allows governments and companies to know a lot more about us than they used to."[2]

Digital identity, digital currencies, contactless society, Internet control, geolocalization, facial recognition, body/machine or brain/machine interfaces to track objects and (human?) livestock, the list of cybernetic threats to the human species could go on for pages. But we won't do it, because they are already available on a search engine or in bookstores. It seems more urgent to bring them back to their overall logic, not always apparent. Indeed, the technical questions are crucial, but do not exhaust the debate. Beyond the involution of positive law in the West or the infinite ramifications of the technostructure, it becomes opportune to talk about lesser-known things, namely the principles of social engineering that organize the thinking of law and the conception of the technostructure. To talk about the concepts that

---

2. HARARI (Yuval), "Every crisis is also an opportunity", in *Le Courrier de l'UNESCO*, 2020, p. 48-53: https://fr.unesco.org/courier/2020-3/yuval-noah-harari-every-crisis-is-opportunity

build the psychological and relational architecture of our surveillance societies. To describe what Big Brother has in his head, and especially how he goes about literally hacking what is in ours.

First of all, let's distinguish between an old and a new Big Brother. The one described by George Orwell in *1984* is still primitive. It is the classic totalitarian figure of political domination: Stalin, Mao, Hitler, Mussolini, and all the traditional potentates. They are in a position of power and everyone knows it. They are seen, placed in the center of attention, with their portraits reproduced in houses, a statue at every traffic circle and their figure omnipresent in the media. It is power in the first degree, the symbolic, patriarchal and inescapable phallus, the totem at the center of the village. The official organization chart of the hierarchy is complete. Maximum visibility, therefore, for the old Big Brother. The new Big Brother is more subtle, because he is invisible. You don't even know he's in power. Worse, you are convinced that it is someone else who is in power, yourself or a fictitious enemy. The official power chart is not complete, there is yet another unofficial power. In *Propaganda*, published in 1928, Edward Bernays already spoke of the "invisible government" of democracies, which is very different from the one that is put forward in the spotlight. The difference between the old and the new Big Brother is simple. The old Big Brother is watching you, and also wants to be watched by you. The new Big Brother is watching you, like the old Big Brother, but unlike the old Big Brother, he doesn't want to be watched by you. Most of his work consists in dissociating the couple "seeing" and "being seen": he sees you, but you don't see him. In terms of political perception, the relationship with the old Big Brother was symmetrical: the dominant and the dominated knew each other as dominant and dominated. With the new Big Brother, the perception is asymmetrical: the dominant still sees the dominated, but the dominated no longer sees the dominant, and may even believe that he does not exist or that he himself is the dominant. The new "democratic" Big Brother is all the more powerful and totalitarian. An invisible power will always be more invasive than a visible power. In 1981, in a controversial interview because of his comments on euthanasia, Jacques Attali anticipated the hygienist dictatorship and the instruments of social control that we see developing today in a coercive manner for medical reasons: "Then, all the medicines of the future that are linked to the control of behavior can have a major political impact. It would indeed be possible to reconcile parliamentary democracy with totalitarianism, since it would be enough to maintain all the formal rules of parliamentary democracy, but at the same time to generalize the use of these products so that totalitarianism would be daily. M.S.: Does this seem conceivable, an Orwellian "1984" based on a pharmacology of behavior? J.A.: I don't believe in Orwellianism, because it is a form of technical totalitarianism with a visible and centralized Big Brother. I believe rather in an implicit totalitarianism with an invisible and decentralized Big Brother. These machines to monitor our health, which we could have for our own good, will enslave us for our own good. In a way, we will undergo a soft and permanent conditioning..."[3]

"Big Brother is watching you. But you are NOT watching it." By taking great care to remain invisible, the new Big Brother is therefore *hacking.* Hacking is the stealthy violation of the integrity of a system. If your computer is hacked, it means that someone has entered it without you seeing it, or too late. But stronger than computer hacking is cognitive hacking, brain infiltration, or neurohacking. The general method of hacking any system, computer or brain is called social

---

3. ATTALI (Jacques), " La médecine en accusation ", in *L'avenir de la vie,* directed by Michel Salomon, Seghers, 1981, p. 272.

engineering. Hacker Kevin Mitnick laid the foundation by showing that the weakest link in security systems is the human factor. In this sense, social engineering is the general method by which a hacker becomes invisible to an attacker, and thus opens up the possibility of stealthily reading and modifying the hacker's source code, i.e. the constants and commands that define his root behavioral program.

In its most negative and destructive version, social engineering proceeds in two steps: a hooking of the prey, a phishing, whose condition of success is the invisibility of the predator in the eyes of the prey; then the destruction of the prey, that is to say its dissolution in a process of indirect accelerated entropy, whose procedure consists in making the contradictions rise in it until the point of rupture. In this way, the prey dies and disappears without ever having understood what was happening to it, or too late. The metaphor of angling is apt. A fish that sees a predator runs away, or defends itself. To deceive the fish's self-preservation instinct, the predator must deceive its vigilance with a hook. The fish must perceive what is going to kill it as harmless, and even as downright good for it and attractive. A false good for a true evil. In fact, the hooked fish has only perceived the maggot, not the hook that is going to kill it or the fisherman on the shore that is going to eat it. The question that the new Big Brother asks himself is always: "How do we occupy the place of the fisherman, invisible to the fish, i.e. how do we occupy the place of the predator invisible to the prey?" The answer is: "By the apparent reversal of roles." The predator poses as prey. The strong pretend to be the weak. To stretch the metaphor, one might say that with his fishing rod as an extension of his arm, the fisherman poses as a maggot. In our victimized age, this means that the predator must occupy the place of the "victim."

The concept of the "dramatic triangle" proposed by psychiatrist Stephen Karpman describes a common three-place structure of social interaction: the victim, the victimizer, the savior. The first stage of social engineering, phishing, is performed by becoming invisible as the predator, which often requires occupying the place of the "victim" or "savior" in the psychosocial imagination and its relational geometry. The second step will consist for the predator in destroying his prey by making the contradictions rise in it, which, applied to the human, means orchestrating and provoking triangulated conflicts between the various social actors of the target system by describing them as mutual "executioners". Organizing the war of all against all, governing by chaos. But a directed chaos.

Mastering the range of trust, indifference and distrust is therefore the key to neurohacking and social engineering. Once you trust me because I am a "victim" or a "savior" in your eyes, you lower your defenses, open yourself up to me and I begin to enter your brain, thus infiltrating the central command post of your defense system. To become invisible as a predator, you need to awaken trust, or failing that, not to awaken anything at all, and therefore to set up a blind spot of indifference behind which I will advance and act with impunity. The second phase, that of the triangulated conflict, will be achieved by awakening distrust between you and the other actors of the target system, described as "executioners" of each other.

To take power and keep it, our new Big Brother applies this method of social engineering in a systematic way. Everyone can see the variations of this method in the media and in the socio-political field, where the same stories and the same language elements are repeated endlessly in a monotonous way, like mantras, with tiny variations on the same theme, in order to try to condition Pavlovian mental reflexes in the population, which is trained to designate a victim, an executioner, a savior... and that's all! An impression of general robotization emerges from all this, which is only apparently

Governing by chaos

contradictory with the production of chaos. Indeed, in order to better automate human behavior, to better program it, plan it, control it, pilot it, mechanize it, there is nothing like plunging it into chaos, i.e. panic. The branch of behaviorism that studies the effects of extreme stress has shown that in situations of great anxiety, of vital urgency, of panic, the reptilian brain and its primary functions prevail over the dialectical neocortex. This sidelining of the complex functions of the brain allows the number of possible behaviors to be reduced to those of survival: instinctive, stereotyped, rigid behaviors, easy to model and predict, and above all short term, short sighted and unplanned, of the "reflex" type, therefore sometimes counter-productive and self-destructive, because they are thoughtless. The reduction of behavioral diversity and complexity is accompanied by a reduction in behavioral uncertainty, and therefore by a better predictability of behavior. To effectively take control of a group, it must never have time to think. The new Big Brother seeks, like the old one, to homogenize our behaviors and to reduce their diversity to unity; but the new one has understood that to achieve this, it is more efficient to rely on disorder and anarchy than on a lucid social order whose stability can turn against the Power itself. The latest developments in criminology point in this direction.

In the methodological arsenal of social engineering, criminology occupies a place of choice, particularly in its so-called actuarial version. Actuarial science is a branch of risk science (cindynics) that consists in calculating the potential dangerousness of an individual or a group and then taking measures in anticipation. This approach in terms of behavioral prediction, which justifies an arrest even before the crime has been committed, was popularized by the film *Minority Report*, adapted from a short story by Philip K. Dick. A detailed description is given by Bernard Harcourt, professor of law, in an interview with the jurist and magistrate Antoine Garapon: "Dangerousness," wrote Robert Castel more than 25 years ago in a premonitory book entitled *La gestion des risques*; "dangerousness," he wrote, "is this mysterious notion, a quality that is immanent to a subject, but whose existence remains uncertain since objective proof is never given until after the fact. The diagnosis that is established is the result of a probability calculation; the dangerousness does not result from a personalized clinical evaluation, but from a statistical calculation that transposes to human behavior the methods developed by the insurance industry to calculate risks. Hence a new science (and remember that word): actuarial science."[4]

Today, criminology no longer aims at arresting criminals, but at standardizing behavior. The penal reform supported in its time by Christiane Taubira, which opens the prisons and puts delinquents and criminals back on the street in exchange for a punctual administrative follow-up, was wrongly qualified as lax. It belongs to the register of anarcho-tyranny, according to the concept of Samuel T. Francis, that form of social control making strategic use of social disorder. Beyond its primary apparent function of producing insecurity, this type of penal reform is also part of an ultra-repressive system aimed at reducing the difference in treatment between what is guilty and what is not. This blurring of the boundaries between real and potential dangerousness, which no longer clearly distinguishes the prison world from the rest of society, is also applied under the pretext of a health emergency in the various measures aimed at treating any individual as if he or she were ill, based on the risk that he or she might become so. Since 2020, the authorities have been playing Dr. Knock and making the healthy internalize that they are potentially

---

4. "La criminologie actuarielle", *France Culture*, April 23, 2008 : https://www.radiofrance.fr/franceculture/podcasts/le-bien-commun-13-14/la-criminologie-actuarielle-3454827

Governing by chaos

sick. On the same principle, actuarial criminology will erode, abrade, abolish the barrier between the acted guilty and the non guilty of the other. These two approaches are both part of the same philosophy aiming at having only sick people and potential guilty people, and semi-freedom for all. These practices of social control have nothing to do with law or health, but belong to the actuarial register, which seeks to dilute and confuse the distinct statuses of pathology and health, on the one hand, and guilt and innocence, on the other, in an undifferentiated "primitive soup" allowing the extension of isolation and confinement measures by prevention, and thus extending the walls of the prison and the quarantine to the whole of society.

Actuarial criminology can be combined with predictive justice, but also with predictive medicine, to try to justify the reversal of the burden of proof. What does this change? We all become suspects or sick *a priori*. Health no longer exists, because you are potentially a "contact case", "healthy carrier" or "asymptomatic", and you must be tested and screened even if you are in good shape. In the legal field, the presumption of innocence is reversed into a presumption of guilt. It is no longer up to the prosecutor to prove that you are guilty, it is up to you to prove that you are innocent. Your "assessed dangerousness" and your "criminal potential" are enough to trigger the judicial machine and to bring down the anti-terrorist brigades on you. The criminal act is no longer necessary, the probability that you will commit it is enough. Worse than the crime of intent is the crime of possible intent. The stratagem to justify the surveillance and self-monitoring of populations in the name of a diffuse, global, paranoid "terrorist threat" is today associated with the "health threat", more efficient, because it flatters the hypochondriac tendencies of each one, and leads to this daily parade of zombies with beaten dogs' heads under their face masks. On its side, terrorism has become endemic and autonomous, it is accomplished by stabbings in the street and does not need anymore the State special services, nor their paramilitary auxiliaries coming to assist them, and which are the only real actors able to organize large-scale attacks, like those of *Charlie Hebdo* or the Bataclan. This disturbing fact will be obvious to anyone who makes the effort to learn a little about the working methods of the special units of the police and the army. The *Gladio* and *Stay Behind* networks, and their "strategy of tension", are still relevant today. A new slogan, "Democratizing the culture of intelligence", must therefore be propagated as widely as possible, so that the true nature of clandestine operations appears in relief and live, at the very moment they take place, and that they no longer deceive anyone.

I therefore accuse the French State of health terrorism, but also of Islamist terrorism. For while individuals are being killed without trial to cover up the truth in attacks with compromising ramifications, the French State is killing in Libya and Syria, where it supports jihadists and other "moderate rebels" doing "good work" and engaged in massacres in the service of the "remodeling of the Greater Middle East" launched by George W. Bush in his speech of February 26, 2003. I also accuse the French state of extreme right-wing terrorism. For while patriotic organizations are demonized and accused of fascism in France, the French state kills in Ukraine where it supports the colorful Maïdan revolution and its neo-Nazi putschists to overthrow the legal government in Kiev in February 2014 and advance NATO's pawns on its grand chessboard towards Moscow. And I finally accuse the French state of far-left terrorism. For, while the Yellow Vests were marching, the French state was infiltrating its police "apparatchiks" disguised as *black blocs* into the demonstrations and into "anti-fascist" leftism in order to push its militants into violence and maintain a strategy of tension favorable to the interests of international capitalism. I therefore accuse the French state of high treason and intelligence with the enemy when it puts itself at the service of foreign interests and governs this country through controlled chaos.

Intuitively, chaos is uncertainty and unpredictability. At first sight, a chaotic subject should therefore be uncertain and unpredictable. The great secret of social engineering is that, contrary to appearances, the more chaotic a subject is, the more predictable it is. A subject immersed in chaos develops only very short-term logic, purely reactive, and therefore easy to guess and anticipate, and he becomes incapable of elaborating an autonomous strategic planning on the long term. On an emotional level, chaos is synonymous with panic. Nothing is more predictable than a panicked subject. Moreover, even if the panicked subject escapes the planned scenario, he or she has not been able to develop his or her own scenario. This is the most important point. In complex systems, it is futile to try to control everything, but one can limit the horizon of possibilities. Real power does not consist in winning the game but in defining the rules of the game.

This book, first published by Max Milo in 2010, invites you to discover the principles of social engineering and governance by chaos. Everything that this booklet announced at the time, including the attempt to reset humanity to implement a transhumanist dictatorship, has been confirmed over time. The introduction to the third edition that you hold in your hands merges the preface of the second edition of 2014 with an article published in 2021, in issue 80 of *Civitas* magazine, and the rest of the text has been revised and expanded. Why did you maintain the author's anonymity for the first two editions and lift it now? Anonymity is a discipline whose goal is to focus on the message rather than the messenger. What is the problem with political debate today? Too much personalization. This is not a coincidence, it is an age-old communication technique that aims to bypass embarrassing facts by shifting the debate to the person reporting them. Nowadays, the facts are systematically embarrassing for the Power, whose real enemy is the Real and which is therefore determined to make diversion on the people who point the facts. "When the finger points at the moon, the fool looks at the finger. In order to hysterize the debate, one will voluntarily speak only about the finger, so as to make everyone stupid. The objective examination of reality is thus replaced by subjective and passionate debates, which lower the level and lock us into the virtuality of the political spectacle. When someone says "2 + 2 = 4", it consists in rephrasing "You think that 2 + 2 = 4". Thus, adding a signature to a fact. Not to sign a text is then the first step of a pedagogy of the return of reality in politics. This was my original intention. As time went by, however, I had to take into account another fact, obvious as soon as one practices a bit of memetics and communication: information that is not transmitted does not exist. Ideas have no intrinsic existence, they only exist because they are spread and carried at arm's length by those who support them, and word of mouth is not always enough. This is the reason for the small change on the cover of the book.

Ordo ab chao

In a November 19, 2008 article in the daily *Libération*, the philosopher Giorgio Agamben summarized the beginnings of the so-called Tarnac affair as follows: "At dawn on November 11, 150 police officers, most of whom belonged to the anti-terrorist brigades, surrounded a village of 350 inhabitants on the Millevaches plateau before entering a farm to arrest nine young people (who had taken over the grocery store and tried to revive the village's cultural life). Four days later, the nine people arrested were brought before an anti-terrorist judge and "accused of criminal association with terrorist intent."[5]

Hooded and armed, the police and gendarmes carried out their operation under the noses of journalists, warned in advance, and of a local population shocked by the intentionally spectacular and traumatic staging. Aged between 23 and 34, the nine individuals arrested in their sleep found themselves under investigation by the Ministry of the Interior for having taken part in the sabotage of SNCF train lines. A political book, entitled *The Coming Insurrection*, written by an

---

5. "Terrorisme ou tragi-comédie", *Libération*, November 19, 2008: https://www.liberation.fr/societe/2008/11/19/terrorisme-ou-tragi-comedie_257959/

anonymous "Invisible Committee" but attributed to this group, was used as evidence by the police. It contains calls for civil disobedience and sabotage of the instruments of power, which links this text to the movement described as ultra-left, which would be highly likely to take action, according to the ministry. But apart from these suppositions, the file remains empty and the material evidence does not jostle to make the accusation credible. A dozen other young people suspected of being linked to this group were arrested the same day elsewhere in the country, but quickly released for lack of evidence. Very quickly, another committee, this one of support, was set up, composed of people close to the accused, family, friends, neighbors, as well as intellectuals and sympathetic journalists. The rather quick accusation of terrorism and the detention without proof which is nevertheless prolonged for several people have scandalized a lot of people, well beyond the militant circles of the extreme left. Other support groups are springing up all over France and even abroad; conferences, concerts and demonstrations are being organized under the slogan: "Let's sabotage antiterrorism!"

On Saturday, January 31, 2009, one of these demonstrations snaked through the streets of Paris through the 5th and 14th arrondissements. A heterogeneous population had previously gathered on the Place Edmond Rostand, the starting point of the march, between the varnished gates of the Luxembourg Gardens and the columns of the Pantheon at the end of the Rue Soufflot. The procession set off in the early afternoon and headed south towards the Santé prison, where Julien Coupat, one of the nine defendants, presented in the media as the leader of the group, was still locked up. All along the route, cordons of CRS blocked the access to the perpendicular streets and channeled the procession in a kind of mousetrap whose goal was to prevent anyone from approaching the prison in numbers. Stopped on the boulevard Arago and realizing too late the scheme, some demonstrators start to send projectiles and to shoot fireworks mortars horizontally at the CRS ; who, protected behind their shields and their grilled trucks, don't risk much anyway...

The demonstration dissolved in about 30 minutes, leaving behind a failed urban riot atmosphere and demolished billboards. Throughout the march, the sound truck with music blaring from it had a mock slogan painted on its side: "Al Qaeda. Yes, it's possible!" Many people carried homemade signs that declared, in essence, "We are all terrorists!" Small white masks, like those of the intern movement, are handed out with the word TERRORIST written on them in marker. In short, everyone is claiming terrorist status. This situation reminds us irresistibly of the last sequence of *V for Vendetta*, when the people take to the streets to storm the Parliament, each face hidden behind a Guy Fawkes mask, the one worn by Anonymous, identical to the one worn by a mysterious lone vigilante that the police and the media accuse of being... a terrorist.

The main thread of the subsequent events will remain for posterity what is indeed agreed to call a "delirious breath" of the French justice system, condemned to flee forward in order not to lose face. In the first days, everything seemed coherent, but quite quickly the case turned out to be empty of evidence and more symptomatic of a disturbing evolution of Power, engaged in a drift of generalized suspicion and in a fantasy of total control. After years of investigation, the file was still empty. No evidence, nothing, nothing. In 2018, the main defendants were finally acquitted and the president of the 14th chamber of the Paris correctional court, Corinne Goetzmann, had this to say: "The hearing made it clear that the Tarnac group was a fiction."[6] But it is

---

6. "Tarnac trial: a quasi-general acquittal sweeps away the erring investigation," *Sud Ouest*, November 12, 2018: https://www.sudouest.fr/justice/proces-tarnac-une-relaxe-quasi-generale-balaie-les-errances-de-l-enquete-3104452.php

Governing by chaos

indeed on the basis of a fiction that the measures of detention and police control piled up without any principle of reality for ten years, that a good twenty people also had to undergo police custody, and that a tenth thief was indicted for having had the misfortune to be a sympathizer of these dangerous grocers. So why? Today, we can ask ourselves: what was the name of the Tarnac affair?

Certainly, particular career interests were probably at play, when intelligence services needed to invent enemies in order not to disappear in fatal restructurings or when a criminology advisor to the Élysée Palace began to see terrorists everywhere to please one of his first employers, the New York City Council. But beyond these little dirty deals, this story seems to us to be the revelation of a real mutation of the political field. One could say that there is apparently nothing new under the sun. Anthropology has taught us that, from time immemorial, power has had to rely on lies and scapegoats to establish its hold. But, the lying strategies of the old order had at least one advantage, that of offering to the dominated majority a space of social and psychic stability. Chaos was the enemy of order. In the 20th century, new forms of social control appeared, which we can gather under the concept of social engineering, and whose object is not only to derealize the public sphere, as in the past, but moreover to destructure intentionally the social body and the individual psyche in the popular classes. Today, chaos is the instrument of order.

This new postmodern, globalized order is the result of an alliance between lies, which are more than ever at the heart of the system, and a certain number of techniques for the programmed deconstruction of socio-cultural balances. The "pyromaniac fireman" is the name of one of these political marketing methods which consists, for example, in creating insecurity upstream in order to create a "demand" for security downstream and to respond to it with a security "offer". Anti-terrorism, as a mode of government based on the diffusion of a fear inducing submission in the popular strata, absolutely needs terrorists, real or fictitious. In both cases, it is necessary to create them, by the maintenance of sociological conditions favorable to their emergence or, failing that, in a totally imaginary way. But no one must know, and everyone must tremble before these new scarecrows and bogeymen - the ultra-left, the extreme right, the Islamists - on which the system is entirely based and without which it would quickly collapse. The "terrorist threat", of which Julien Coupat and his friends have been accused, is completely in line with this device which allows to criminalize almost anyone who does not think correctly. Such as Varg Vikernes, the Norwegian musician who settled in 2013 in a village of Corrèze - also after having served a prison sentence in his native country - and suspected of being a survivalist, doubled with a neo-pagan white supremacist, therefore of harboring bad right-wing thoughts - to vary a bit. The accusation of "sectarian and conspiratorial drift", which appeared in 2021 in a Miviludes document, will make it possible to classify real "sectarian and conspiratorial drift" in a catch-all category with blurred limits, alongside individuals who apply Cartesian doubt to the political and media discourse, or who can no longer bear the hell of modern cities and wish to settle down in the countryside in autonomy. The purely media accusation sometimes authorizes the Power to kill arbitrarily and without trial. In a state governed by the rule of law, the guilt of an accused person emerges during a fair and contradictory trial in which evidence of guilt is brought forward if it exists. It seems that this has become superfluous in the treatment of certain "terrorists", whether in France or in Guantanamo. For all those who are killed during their arrest, we will never know if they acted independently, or if they had the green light from their handlers, or if they are collateral damage of an internal war between police services. Such was the case of an informer named Mohammed Merah, who traveled to Israel, Turkey, Syria, Jordan, Pakistan, Afghanistan, under the watchful eye of intelligence services that sacrificed him after use.[7]

Our object of study is this methodical and planned involution, the analysis of which was inaugurated in the insurrectionary work already cited. What has happened to those who have associated themselves too closely with this text only confirms this. The political ideal, exposed in the tract *Mise au point*, distributed during a winter demonstration in 2009, is reaffirmed here at least in the perspective of "collectivizing" the accusation, of mutualizing it and extending it to the maximum so as to make it unmanageable by the power, unless it reveals its true intentions, namely the incarceration of the whole population, revealing by this very fact its true nature. Yes, there is "an order to bring down". Destroy in order to rule, this is the motto of this New World Order based on chaos and that we must overthrow. Destroying those who destroy in order to rule is therefore at this stage simply self-defense.

Politics and massification

The definition of a relevant defense strategy requires a good knowledge of the enemy in order to discover its strong points, which can be circumvented, and its points of vulnerability, which can be attacked. To this end, we must take up the theories of "risk management", which allows us to identify the weaknesses as well as the

---

7. "How Mohamed Merah "became" an informant for the "services"", *Slate*, March 27, 2012: https://www.slate.fr/story/52297/mohamed-merah-informateur

vulnerabilities of any system. And to begin with, describe the theater of operations, as precisely as possible, before acting.

From the general to the particular, the state of affairs seems to begin with the following observation: in the context of mass societies, politics is always more or less an activity of social control exercised by dominant minorities over dominated majorities. There is no reason to rejoice in this, but it seems that beyond a certain demographic threshold, the political ideal of direct, participatory and self-managing democracy must give way to the system of representation, with all the phenomena of elite confiscation of power that are consubstantial with it. The nature of this social control of the masses, long synonymous with concrete political practice, has nevertheless undergone profound changes over time, especially in the 20th century. Indeed, from the 1920s onwards, the scientific study of human behavior began to take the place of religion and philosophy as the foundation of this political practice. For the first time in human history, the Prince's advisor was no longer debating ideas from a podium or a book, but was dealing with stimuli in a laboratory. This change of method gave birth to or was consolidated by new disciplines such as marketing, management, cybernetics, which are grouped under the term management sciences, and which thus became the new instruments of political practice and social control. Thus, from an activity of inculcation of a system of values - a law, divine or republican -, politics has moved towards the purely technical questions of engineering behavior and optimizing the management of groups. Thanks to these new tools, the political elites of industrialized countries have thus been able to dispense with any form of axiology, of discussion about values, ideas, meaning and principles, in order to devote themselves solely to the organizational technology of populations.

In the space of a few decades, developed countries have thus gone from a social control based on language, interlocution, the linguistic summoning of humans and the activation of their symbolization functions, to a social control based on the behavioral programming of the masses by means of emotional manipulation and physical coercion. And under this impulse, as Bernard Stiegler remarks, human societies are passing from a symbolized superego, the Law in the general sense, to an automated superego, the pure technological constraint, after a transition by a kind of "emotional superego" emanating from the Spectacle.

In other words, politics, which was once the art of regulating the contradictions of a group by inculcating in its members a common Law, a structuring social grammar allowing exchange beyond disagreements, has today become the art of automating behavior without discussion. The symbolic function, that is to say the capacity of rationalization of emotions and dialectical articulation of their contradictions in a shared discourse, the capacity to continue to speak to each other when we do not agree, keystone of the elaboration of the common sense of an organized group and of the weaving of the social link, is directly attacked by this mutation. If the human subject is indeed a "speaking subject" as psychoanalysis indicates, a being of Word, of Speech, of dialectic, therefore also of polemic, then we can say that these new instruments of the political practice allow us to simply make the economy of the subjectivity and to reduce a group of subjects to a set of objects.

Politics, *Great Reset* and Globalization

Jacques Attali, one of the finest socio-political observers of our time, never ceases to remind us, whether in his writings or in his media interventions: most contemporary leaders have only two fundamental goals, the first being to set up a world government; the second, in order to protect this world government from being overthrown by its enemies, being to create a globalized technical system of generalized surveillance based on the total traceability of objects and persons, reduced to the state of objects. Indeed, in the global cybernetic system, connected subjects become connected objects. This computer surveillance system is already very advanced thanks to artificial intelligence, mobile telephony and the ever-increasing number of cameras and facial recognition devices in our cities. All of this is part of the fourth industrial revolution, announced in 2017 by the World Economic Forum (WEF), the union of big capitalism, better known as the "Davos Forum." An article on its website explains what our future will be made of: "In the First Industrial Revolution, water and steam mechanized production. The Second Industrial Revolution harnessed electrical power to create mass production. The Third Industrial Revolution used electronics and information technology to automate production. The Fourth Industrial Revolution is the result: it is the digital revolution, born in the middle of the last century. It is characterized by a fusion of technologies that blurs the boundaries between the physical, digital and biological spheres. [At the same time, digital manufacturing technologies interact daily with the biological world. Engineers, designers and architects are combining computer design, additive manufacturing, materials engineering and synthetic biology to create a symbiosis between microorganisms, our bodies, the products we consume and even the buildings we live in. [The Fourth Industrial Revolution will not only change what we do, but also who we are. It will affect who we are and all the issues associated with it: our sense of privacy, our notion of ownership, our consumption patterns, the time we spend on work and leisure, the way we develop our careers and skills, the way we meet and maintain relationships. It is already changing our health and leading to a "quantified" notion of self, and it could lead us faster than we think to an augmented human being. The infinite list of possibilities is limited only by our imagination."[8]

In 2020, the president of the World Economic Forum, Klaus Schwab, welcomed the "health crisis" of the coronavirus as a gas pedal of this fourth transhumanist industrial revolution, allowing the Great *Reset* of the human species as if it were a computer to be rebooted. In fact, cybernetics and computer science continue to progress and to frame our lives ever more closely. RFID (Radio Frequency IDentification) technology and body implants of signal-emitting electronic components will eventually ensure our permanent geolocation. This sort of digital tattoo, more than indelible, since it is buried in our flesh in the form of miniaturized chips down to the nanometer, will also contain sufficient biographical and biometric information to authorize remote profiling of its wearer and thus allow anticipation of any behavior assessed as potentially risky on his part. A step forward will soon be taken with the generalization of body-machine or brain-machine interfaces on which many laboratories around the world are working. The CNRS commented on the possibilities offered by graphene as follows: "These results confirm the exceptional qualities of graphene as an interface between the world of electronics and the world of life.

---

8. "The Fourth Industrial Revolution: what it means and how to deal with it," World Economic Forum, October 25, 2017: https://fr.weforum.org/agenda/2017/10/la-quatrieme-revolution-industrielle-ce-qu-elle-implique-et-comment-y-faire-face/

This coating method can be applied to many objects, both two- and three-dimensional, and could significantly reduce the rejection of neural probes or other implants used in many medical fields."[9]

How to convince humans to be injected into their bodies with graphene or related materials such as graphene oxide? A *prerequisite* for starting to develop a vast system of subjects directly connected to cyberspace. In 2021, the Foundation for Research in Chemistry summarized the state of research as follows: "Researchers from the CNRS and the University of Strasbourg have conducted a critical analysis of the most promising strategies based on the use of graphene-related materials reported in the literature to fight viral pandemics such as Covid-19. This perspective was published in the journal *Advanced Materials*."[10]

This computer dictatorship in progress will make it possible to satisfy the fantasy of ubiquitous security of political power, whose ambitions are today limited to an unbridled and paranoid search for zero risk. Globalist integration, as a political project imposed by certain elites on populations, is thus nothing more than the implementation of a vast system of predictability of the behaviors of these populations, in other words a system of total control of counter-powers. There is, in fact, an equivalence between unpredictability and power, as Michel Crozier and Erhard Friedberg note in a seminal work on the sociology of organizations: "[...] the only way I can prevent others from treating me as a means, as a mere thing, is to make my behavior unpredictable, that is, to exercise power. [Within the framework of the simplest

---

9. "A graphene blanket to reduce inflammation caused by neural implants," CNRS, October 29, 2019: https://inp.cnrs.fr/fr/cnrsinfo/une-couverture-de-graphene-pour-reduire-linflammation-causee-par-les-implants-neuronaux?fbclid=IwAR3DALgyN29E-jP-inwdTohqiapls7_anC8JXDIiOk1xnMPYt0oNzBEkPH9A
10. "Fighting Covid-19 and Future Pandemics with Graphene," Foundation for Chemical Research: https://icfrc.fr/combattre-la-covid-19-and-future-pandemics-with-graphene/

power relationship, such as we have been able to discover underlying any organizational situation, we have shown that negotiation can be reconstructed in logic from a reasoning on predictability. Each party seeks to lock the other into a predictable line of reasoning, while retaining the freedom of its own behavior. The one who wins, the one who can manipulate the other, and thus orient the relationship to his or her advantage, is the one who has more leeway. It is as if predictability and inferiority were equivalent.[11]

These political power issues are part of a social class struggle. American billionaire Warren Buffett told the *New York Times* in 2006, "There is a class war, to be sure, but it's my class, the rich class, that's fighting the war and we're winning."[12] In 2009, Warren Buffet was meeting with some very rich friends to talk about demographic control of the poor. The British edition of the *Times* reported on the meeting, which has become known as the *Good Club*: "Some of America's leading billionaires met in secret to consider how their wealth could be used to slow the growth of the world's population and accelerate improvements in health and education. The philanthropists, who attended a summit hosted by Microsoft co-founder Bill Gates, discussed joining forces to overcome political and religious barriers to change. Described as the "right club" by one insider, it included David Rockefeller Jr, the patriarch of America's richest dynasty, Warren Buffett and George Soros, the financiers, Michael Bloomberg, the mayor of New York City, and media moguls Ted Turner and Oprah Winfrey."[13]

---

11. Crozier (Michel) and Friedberg (Erhard), *L'Acteur et le Système*, Le Seuil, 1977, p. 105 and 171.
12. "In Class Warfare, Guess Which Class Is Winning," *New York Times*, November 26, 2006: http://www.nytimes.com/2006/11/26/business/yourmoney/26every.html
13. "Billionaire club in bid to curb overpopulation," *The Times*, May 24, 2009: https://www. thetimes.co.uk/article/billionaire-club-in-bid-to-curb-overpopulation-d2fl22qhl02

Let us now detail these tools with which power has equipped itself to ensure a definitive superiority over the populations by ensuring the total predictability of their behavior and the control of their demography.

What is social engineering?

The culture of inequality does not only concern the economic field. It also affects the configuration of the perceptual field. Indeed, the foundation of surveillance theories, as summarized by Jeremy Bentham's panoptic principle, is the dissociation of the couple "seeing and being seen". Politics as social engineering consists then in building and maintaining an unequal system where some see without being seen, and where others are seen without seeing. The aim of the maneuver is to take control of the system of perception of others without being perceived oneself, and then to produce effects by rewriting the relations of cause and effect in such a way that others are mistaken when they try to reconstruct them in order to understand their present situation. In her book on Nicolas Sarkozy's presidential campaign in 2007, Yasmina Reza reports these words from one of his advisors, Laurent Solly: "[...] reality is not important. It is only the perception that counts.[14] This radical constructivism, originating from the Palo Alto school and very much in vogue in the consulting world, does not hesitate to consider that perception can be detached from any objective, real referent. The engineering of perceptions then becomes a quasi demiurgic activity of construction of collective hallucinations, shared, normalized and defining the

---

14. REZA (Yasmina), *L'Aube, le soir ou la nuit*, Flammarion, 2007, p. 44.

common reality, in other words a stabilized set of falsified causal relations. As the famous hacker Kevin Mitnick argues in an essay, social engineering is the art of deception; more precisely, the art of misleading others and of exercising power over them by playing on the failures and blind spots of their system of perception and defense. Illusionism and prestidigitation applied to the whole social field, so as to build a space of life in trompe-l'oeil, a rigged reality whose true rules have been intentionally camouflaged.

These manipulation techniques are based on the management sciences, a nebulous group of disciplines that began to constitute a coherent corpus in the 1920s and whose information theory and cybernetics summarize the main ideological lines, according to which living beings and conscious subjects are information systems that can be modeled, controlled, and even hacked in the same way as non-living information systems composed of non-conscious objects. For the best known, these management disciplines are marketing, management, robotics, cognitivism, social and behavioral psychology, neuro-linguistic programming (NLP). What these disciplines have in common is their relationship to uncertainty, which they always try to reduce to a minimum, if possible to zero. The world is thus perceived solely from the point of view of information exchange and processing systems that must be managed as well as possible, i.e. by reducing the uncertainty of their functioning, by controlling them as precisely as possible. Moreover, unlike the human and social sciences, these management sciences are not content to observe and describe their object of study, they also intervene on it in the sense of engineering, i.e., a work of reconfiguration of a given. When it is done without the knowledge of the reconfigured system, the reconfiguration becomes a stealthy violation of the integrity of the system and is called *hacking*. And when it is applied to humans, this pirate reconfigurative interventionism generally aims at reconfiguring the human given in the sense of reducing the uncertainty linked to the behavior of this human given, whether individual or group.

Politics as social engineering, management of human masses, reduction of the uncertainty of the behavior of the populations, is thus based first of all on a descriptive phase, constituted by works of modeling of these popular behaviors in order to define the general structures and the constants. This modeling work brings to light the programs, routines, psychological conditioning and behavioral algorithms that human groups obey. Computer science is the ideal tool, for example in the complex calculation (probabilistic and stochastic) of crowd movements, which is used for risk management in professional health and safety authorities (evacuation of buildings), but also by the police and the army to control and prevent any demonstration that might destabilize power. Moreover, the work of spying on a population, with a view to modelling what it thinks and thus defusing new critical tendencies, requires a work of surveillance, intelligence, information gathering and filing that is considerably facilitated by the developments of ubiquitous or ambient and diffuse computing in the environment, as theorized by Mark Weiser, as well as by the "expert systems" of crossing local, public and private electronic databases (interception of communications, card payments, etc.). The cross-referencing of this information gleaned from digital networks allows for the calculation of an estimate of the level of danger that a population (or an individual) represents for the authorities. It is therefore understandable that the computerization of society, in order to bring as many elements of people's lives as possible under its control, is a priority for contemporary politics.

Researchers such as Vance Packard and Éric Sadin have been pioneers in describing these new forms of power that are no longer punitive, but anticipatory, and whose hold is strictly coextensive with that of the technological sphere. Today, international public opinion seems to be animated by a movement of rebellion. The "zero Covid" policy in China has caused so much social unrest that the Chinese government resolved in December 2022 to abandon not only its coercive "health measures" but also the method of institutionally rigging the figures that has been applied internationally for years. In France, the Minister Olivier Véran thus answered on November 4, 2020 in the National Assembly commission to a question from the deputy Jean-Pierre Door on the inclusion in the official statistics of Covid-19 of unproven cases: "In EPHAD, if there was a Covid case in the EPHAD, and therefore there was an epidemic identified in the EPHAD, and a death was suspected Covid, it was identified and recognized as Covid, we did not do a post-mortem PCR test, if that is your question. "[15] Here again we see the demiurgic function of speech, capable of creating a parallel world of representations superimposed on the real world of facts, and allowing a serious problem to be invented entirely with words, on the basis of isolated cases renamed "epidemic" and cases only suspected, but identified as "recognized". This writing game allows to build a virtual "sanitary crisis" by means of simple elements of language and without even going through an experimental screening test, thus in defiance of the most elementary science.[16] And this without forgetting that the tests also contribute to falsify reality with

15. "Response from the Minister of Health to my question about the #COVID19 diagnosis at the death of some very elderly people who never contracted it. #commissiondenquete," Jean-Pierre Door, Twitter, November 5, 2020.https://twitter.com/doorjean/status/1324294666150445056

16. "Impact, management and consequences of the Covid 19 epidemic: Mr. Olivier Véran, Minister of Solidarity and Health. National Assembly video portal, Committees/ Wednesday, November 4, 2020."https://videos.assemblee-nationale.fr/video.9812370_5fa2c74e08d55.impact-gestion-et-consequences-de-lepidemie-du-covid-19--m-olivier-veran-ministre-des-solidarit-4-novembre-2020

their percentage of "false positive" results. If China has put an end to these semantic tricks to justify its health dictatorship, its system of digital surveillance of individuals called "social credit" is still active and gives ideas to the whole world. In fact, spying on the population is not unique to authoritarian or totalitarian regimes. In France, the Ministry of National Education has been engaged in scouring its Internet discussion forums for years, subcontracted in 2008 by the opinion strategy firm I&E (which became Burson Cohn & Wolfe in 2018). The call for tenders for 2009 included the following missions: "Identify strategic themes (perennial, predictable or emerging). Identify and analyze strategic or opinion-forming sources. Identify opinion leaders and whistleblowers and analyze their potential for influence and their ability to form a network. Decipher the sources of debates and their modes of propagation. Identify significant information (especially weak signals). Track significant information over time. Collect quantitative indicators (volume of contributions, number of comments, audience, etc.). Reconcile and interpret this information. Anticipate and evaluate the risks of contagion and crisis. Alert and recommend accordingly. The relevant significant information is that which prefigures a debate, a potential "opinion risk", a crisis or any future high point in which the departments would be involved. [...] Internet monitoring will focus on strategic online sources: sites that "comment" on current events, claims, information, participation, politics, etc. It will thus focus on the online media, the sites of unions, political parties, thematic or regional portals, the militant sites of associations, protest or alternative movements, opinion leaders. The monitoring will also cover generalist search engines, general public and specialized forums, blogs, personal pages, social networks, as well as online appeals and petitions, and other distribution formats (videos, etc.). Formal information sources such as print media, news agency dispatches, specialized trade press, assembly debates, public reports, barometers, studies and polls will also be monitored and processed. Interactions between sources of different nature, the passage of relay from one media to another will be carefully analyzed. [...] The keystone of the monitoring system, the switch to "alert mode" will aim to systematically transmit strategic information or weak signals likely to rise in an unusually accelerated manner."[17]

The Ministries of Health, Justice, and the Interior also use the services of companies offering the same services. Once a sufficient level of population modelling has been achieved, it is possible to move on to the second phase, the engineering work itself, which builds on these discovered models to reconfigure them in the direction of increased standardisation, and thus better predictability of behaviour. Political-social engineering consists of nothing more and nothing less than a work of programming and conditioning of behaviors, or rather of reprogramming and reconditioning, since one never starts from a *tabula rasa*, but always from an already given culture of the group in question, with its own routines and conditioning. Human societies, as information systems, can thus be reconfigured in the sense of harmonization, homogenization, standardization of norms and procedures, in order to give those who manage them a better overview and better control, the ideal being to manage to merge the multitude of heterogeneous human groups into a single global group, a single information system. Centralized administration and secure management: the architects of globalization have no other goals.

---

17. Ministry of National Education, Delegation for Communication, Special Conditions, CCP No. 2008/57 of October 15, 2008: http://www.fabula.org/actualites/documents/26772.pdf

Shock strategy

Social engineering as a work of reconfiguration of a human given always proceeds by inflicting methodical shocks. Indeed, reconfiguring a system to make it more secure and predictable requires first erasing its current mode of configuration. The reinitialization of a human group thus requires provoking its amnesia through a founding trauma, opening a window of action on the group's memory and allowing an external intervener to work on it in order to reformat it, rewrite it, recompose it. The expression *"Shock Doctrine"* to designate this method of social hacking was popularized by Naomi Klein in her 2007 book and in her 2009 film of the same name on "disaster capitalism". The author highlights the homology of the modus operandi of liberal capitalism and scientific torture as theorized in CIA manuals - with a lot of psychiatric references to trauma therapy - namely the intentional production of regressive shocks, in the form of planned economic crises and/or methodical emotional traumas, in order to annihilate the given structures until a clean slate is achieved in order to implant new ones.

The crises that have been provoked, or at least instrumentalized, whether they be health or economic, are part of the arsenal of these great maneuvers of refoundation through destruction, which most often aim to centralize a system more in order to simplify its management. "The American and European banks were not victims of the financial crisis that broke out in the United States in 2008, but are guilty of having deliberately provoked it," said the Center for Public Integrity, an American investigative journalism organization, in May 2009.[18] For his part, economist F. William Engdahl describes on his

---

18. "Des banques coupables d'avoir provoqué la crise financière", *La Presse*, May 7, 2009: https://www.lapresse.ca/affaires/economie/services-financiers/200905/06/01-853948-les-banques-coupables-de-la-crise-selon-une-etude.php

blog the ins and outs of a programmed phenomenon: "Using panic to centralize power. As I discuss in my forthcoming book, *Power of Money: The Rise and Decline of the American Century,* in every major financial panic in the United States since at least 1835, the titans of Wall Street, especially JP Morgan prior to 1929, deliberately set off the banking panic behind the scenes to consolidate their hold on the U.S. banking system. The private banks used the panic to control Washington policy, including the exact definition of private ownership of the new Federal Reserve in 1913, and to consolidate their control over industrial groups like US Steel, Caterpillar, Westinghouse, etc. In short, they are used to this kind of financial warfare, which increases their power. Now they need to do something similar on a global scale so that they can continue to dominate global finance, the heart of the power of the U.S. century."[19]

We know the story of the computer developer who distributed viruses himself in order to sell anti-virus software to the owners of infected computers. In the economic field, we also speak of deregulation or liberalization to euphemistically evoke these intentional destructurations. Naomi Klein gives many examples, supported by Milton Friedman's theoretical reflections, including his famous sentence of 1982, "Only a crisis - real or supposed - can produce changes", which all converge in the aim of destroying national, local or even smaller-scale economies, by deregulating and liberalizing them, in order to re-regulate them by placing them under the tutelage of private multinational companies or transnational organizations such as the International Monetary Fund (IMF). Each time it is a question of making an entity lose its sovereignty, its *self-control*, in order to put

---

19. ENGDAHL (F. William), "Behind the Panic: Financial Warfare over Global Bank Power", 10 October 2008: http://www.engdahl.oilgeopolitics.net/Financial_Tsunami/Warfare_Behind_Panic/warfare_behind_panic.html

it under external control. The major obstacle to this colonial process is the entity's level of health, synonymous in politics with its level of autonomy and sovereignty, which naturally resists this attempt at reconfiguration through a foreign takeover, this "hostile takeover" felt as an alienation and a transgression of its integrity. The violence of the shocks inflicted will be commensurate with the level of health and sovereignty of the entity, its level of resistance.

Moreover, in a social engineering framework, the shocks inflicted need not always be real; they can be dramatized only in the field of perceptions. Methodical shocks can therefore be pure hoaxes and illusions, or they can mix reality and illusion, as Alain Minc notes in *Dix jours qui ébranleront le monde*: "Only a traumatic event will wake us up, so much so that the effect of September 11, 2001, has vanished. It could be a false alarm in London, the appearance of a cybervirus likely to block the world's computer networks, or worse, the act of a psychopath who values himself according to the number of his victims. Democracies never anticipate but they react. The public opinion forbids preventive measures that would disrupt daily life, but it accepts the decisions that follow a traumatic event. Nothing would be better, to put us on the alert, than a gigantic hoax, as soon as it has caused a panic: a false nuclear blackmail would therefore be a good pedagogy.[20]

Change management

Resistance to change is the main problem to overcome in social engineering. The question that always arises for the practitioner is: "How to provoke the least resistance to my reconfiguration work,

---

20. MINC (Alain), *Dix jours qui ébranleront le monde*, Grasset, 2009, p. 122.

how to ensure that the shocks inflicted do not provoke a reaction of rejection?" So how to make people accept the change, and if possible how to make them want it, how to make them adhere to the shocks and the reformatting that follows? How to make people like instability, movement, precariousness, "bougism"? In short, how to inoculate entire populations with Stockholm syndrome? A prelude consists in preparing minds by promoting in the public space key words such as nomadism, dematerialization, deterritorialization, mobility, flexibility, rupture, reforms, etc. But this is by no means sufficient. In all cases, direct attack, whose visibility causes a counter-productive reactive cabrage, must be abandoned in favor of indirect tactics, known as circumvention in the military vocabulary (Sun Tzu, Liddell Hart).

In terms of management and sociology of organizations, this strategy of indirect shock is called "change management" or "directed change". Issue 645 of the weekly magazine *Charlie Hebdo* reports these remarks by Renaud Dutreil, then Minister of the Civil Service, made on October 20, 2004 at a Fondation Concorde luncheon-debate on the theme of "How to instill change": "Like all right-wing politicians, I was impressed by the opponent. But I think that we were considerably overestimating this force of resistance. What counts in France is psychology, unlocking all these psychological locks. [The problem we have in France is that people are happy with public services. The hospital works well, the school works well, the police work well. So we have to talk about it, explain that we are on the verge of a major crisis, which is what Michel Camdessus does so well, but without panicking people, because then they will cower like turtles." [21]

---

21. VEIL (Emmanuelle), "Réforme de l'État : Renaud Dutreil se lâche", *Charlie Hebdo*, October 27, 2004: http://filinfo.joueb.com/news/reforme-de-l-etat-renaud-dutreil-se-lache

The method illustrated by these words sums up the spirit of social engineering - to make a group change when it does not feel the need to do so because, overall, it works for it - and the method itself: the intentional dysfunctioning of what works well, but which we do not control, in order to replace it with something we do control; in this case, the destruction of public services that work well, but which escape speculation and the market, in order to replace them with privatized services funded by speculation. We must admit the success of this plan announced in 2004: French public services that were working well at the time will be on their last legs in 2023. Since the presidential mandate of Nicolas Sarkozy, confirmed by those of François Hollande and Emmanuel Macron, France has been the object of a total, methodical and meticulous destruction of its social and economic structures, as well as of its political and cultural structures, a destruction accompanied by a major effort to manufacture the consent of its population to an unprecedented degradation of its living conditions in order to align them with those of liberal globalization. In the past, destruction on such a scale, on the scale of a nation, required a coup d'état or a military invasion. (This is what the executive branch seems to fear, since a February 2007 revision of the criminal statute of the head of state abandoned the expression high treason for that of failure to perform duties manifestly incompatible with the exercise of his mandate). Nowadays, a well-conducted change management process achieves the same thing as a putsch or a war, but without a blow, by gradual and small touches, by segmenting and individualizing the impacted population, so that the overall perception of the project is blurred and the reaction is made more difficult. Thus, Denis Kessler, former vice-president of the Mouvement des entreprises de France (MEDEF), wrote in *Challenges* magazine in October 2007: "The French social model is the pure product of the

Conseil national de la Résistance. A compromise between Gaullists and Communists. It is high time to reform it, and the government is working on it. The government's successive announcements of various reforms may give the impression of a patchwork quilt, as they seem so varied, of unequal importance and diverse in scope: the status of the civil service, special pension schemes, the overhaul of social security, parity... On closer inspection, it becomes clear that there is a profound unity to this ambitious program. The list of reforms? It's simple: take everything that was put in place between 1944 and 1952, without exception. It is there. It is a question today of getting out of 1945, and methodically undoing the program of the National Council of the Resistance!"[22]

Other names can be used to describe this method: strategy of tension, firefighting, order from chaos, creative destruction, "dissolve and coagulate", or the problem-reaction-solution trilogy. Kurt Lewin and Thomas Moriarty, two founders of social psychology, theorized this method in three stages in the articulation between what they called "freezing effect" and "fluidification". The freezing effect describes the spontaneous tendency of human beings not to change their habits and internal structures of functioning, to maintain their *"habitus"*, a tendency which is at the basis of all culture and all tradition as a set of ordered habits, specific to a group and transmitted identically between generations. The fluidification designates the action outside the group consisting in throwing the disorder in its culture and its traditions, creating tensions with the aim of destructuring its habits of functioning and of dislocating this group in more or less short term. Weakened and vulnerable, its immune defenses compromised

---

22. KESSLER (Denis), "Adieu 1945, raccrochons notre pays au monde !", *Challenges*, October 4, 2007: https://www.challenges.fr/magazine/adieu-1945-raccrochons-notre-pays-au-monde-l-editorialiste_338714

and its level of sovereignty lowered, the group can then be rebuilt on the basis of new imported norms, which implant an exogenous type of regulation allowing it to take control from the outside.

The famous phrase of Jean Monnet, one of the founding fathers of the European Union, "Men accept change only when it is necessary and they see necessity only in a crisis", could serve as a maxim for all social engineers. A well-managed change management process consists of three steps: to fluidify the "frozen" structures of the group by the injection of disturbing factors and disruptive elements leading to a crisis - this is stage 1 of the creation of the problem, the intentional destruction or "controlled demolition" ; this destabilization inevitably provokes a reaction of disarray in the group - this is stage 2, the difficulty of which consists in carefully dosing the disturbances provoked, a total panic risking to make the system escape the control of the experimenter; finally, stage 3, a solution of restabilization is brought to the group, a heteronomous solution that the group will welcome with enthusiasm to calm its anguish, without realizing that, by doing so, it has given itself over to an external interference.

Social learning

Change management as a technique for taking control of a group is naturally linked to *social learning,* an English expression that could be translated as the re-education of the masses. In order to explain what this approach consists of, we will start with a long but perfectly explicit quote from Éric Denécé, the founder of the French Center for Research on Intelligence (CF2R): "*Social Learning* uses the combined effects of culture, knowledge and psychology to lead a targeted population to reason according to a certain thought pattern initiated by the influencer, for political, economic or socio-cultural purposes. *Social Learning* is therefore a social formatting for influence purposes. Its objective is the conquest of "mental territories". Through *Social Learning*, economic actors seek to take control of a market, upstream, by shaping its tastes and needs - even by conditioning them - and finally by imposing its products, which then seem to respond naturally to its expectations. It is a question of adapting, sometimes long in advance, the customer to its offer, of destroying that of the competition, but also of substituting the political and cultural influence of its State for that of rival nations. In the information age, gunboat diplomacy is thus replaced by intellectual influence. [...] What he is aiming at are the decision-making or reference centers of a nation - administrative, political, economic, cultural, sports, musical, etc. - that have the power to decide, to influence, to influence, to influence. - This maneuver then directs, in all likelihood, the direction of the community's development. This maneuver then legitimately orients the targeted public towards the offer hidden behind this apparently innocuous training process. It is a matter of conquering hearts and minds well in advance of commercial opportunities. [...] The origins of *Social Learning*. Even before the end of the Second World War, when the Allies had won the war, the British and the Americans wondered how best to avoid a new conflict with Germany. The solution was to create a collusion of values between the three countries. Links were forged with the future German elite in order to establish an exchange of ideas. Thus, in Wilton Park, a manor near London, the Anglo-Americans organized meetings in 1944 with the aim of educating the German elites who were to succeed Hitler in an Anglo-Saxon vision of the world based on democracy and economic liberalism. This was intended to extract them from their "Germanness" and turn them into "civilized" beings, according to Anglo-American standards. Such an initiative was reinforced by the Marshall Plan (1947), and then by the important American presence in the framework of NATO. It led to the lasting attachment of Federal Germany to Western Europe and to Atlanticism." [23]

Social learning is thus devoted to the intentional modification of the way of life, the habits and customs of a given human group, without its knowledge and by letting it believe that it is a natural evolution. For example, the rural exodus and the concentration of populations in cities, typical phenomena of globalization, always presented as historical inevitabilities, in reality respond to two objectives: one economic, to cut off human groups from their food autonomy to make them totally dependent on industrial suppliers and seed companies of genetically modified organisms (Monsanto, Limagrain); the other, political, to facilitate surveillance, which is easier in urban areas than in the countryside. This convergence of interests and methods of the market and politics began to be elaborated and concerted from the 1920s onwards, as analyzed by Stuart Ewen, historian of advertising. Drawing on abundant quotations from their writings and press statements, Ewen shows how American industrialists and social scientists thought together, in the aftermath of the First World War, about how to create a new kind of society and a new kind of individual exclusively oriented to production and consumption. He summarizes their reflections as follows: "To create a national culture and to give it coherence through the social bond of consumption is a project that is fundamentally a matter of 'social planning.' [...] Traditional family structures, rural lifestyles, and immigrant ethical codes had largely shaped the attitudes of the working classes in America. [...] The subjectivity of traditional culture impeded

---

23. FRANÇOIS (Ludovic), DENECE (Éric), HARBULOT (Christian), *Business sous influence*, Éditions d'Organisation, 2004, p. 64-65.

the march of machinism towards the coming synthesis promised by the new order of industrial culture. It was up to industry to give shape to this new order by arranging to liquidate the old." [24]

Social learning thus refers to directed change based on the "manufacture of consent" to change. It is an indirect strategy of behavioral pressure aimed at defusing upstream any resistance to change and to the troubles it causes by camouflaging any strategic intention against which to resist, so that the conscious steering of the group remains unconscious to the latter, imperceptible and attributed to a natural evolution of societies for which nobody is responsible. *"There is no alternative"*, as Margaret Thatcher used to say. Concealing any trace of will in the process of change is essential to make people accept the shocks by provoking as little reaction as possible, except perhaps nostalgia and depressed comments about decadence and human nature being bad. Fatalism, resignation, submission and passivity are expected. It is imperative that the subject being piloted be as little aware as possible of the existence of the pilot and the pilot, so that he cannot even think of interfering in the mechanism to play an active role. To this end, it seems necessary to make it impossible for the piloted subject to have access to an overall vision of the system in which he finds himself, a global vision of overhang, general and systemic, which would allow him to go back to the primary causes of the situation. This scrambling operation, which is nothing else than a hacking of the subject's system of perception and analysis, will consist in specializing his capacities of reasoning and in fragmenting them on particular tasks, so as to direct their focus in a direction which remains harmless for the power.

---

24. EWEN (Stuart), *Consciences under influence - Advertising and the genesis of the consumer society*, Culture&Racines, 2022, p. 98, 102.

Manufacture of consent

The hacking of a subject in order to obtain his consent can also be based on an induced mental regression. This technique implies, in the first instance, addressing only the emotions and affectivity. Noam Chomsky and Edward Herman have made the expression "manufacture of consent" famous, but it was Edward Bernays (1891-1995) who invented it. Nephew of Freud, great reader of Gustave Le Bon and his *Psychology of the crowds*, the man embodies the transfer of competences between marketing and politics, and the blurring of the limit between both. It was under his impetus that politics began to take as its model the analysis of *feedback from* consumer behavior in supermarkets, banks, insurance companies and personalized services, as well as the implementation of solutions that optimize their management: market analysis, audience segmentation, definition of a core target, artificial creation of new needs, etc. Founder of modern propaganda, which he renamed "public relations consulting" to improve its image, Bernays not only invented various advertising techniques, but also orchestrated campaigns to destabilize Latin American governments for the CIA. What distinguishes democratic regimes from dictatorships is now simply a question of method, which is more subtle in a democracy, since it manages to shape people's opinions without them even realizing it. As Bernays himself says in his 1928 seminal work *Propaganda*, "the conscious, intelligent manipulation of the opinions and organized habits of the masses plays an important role in a democratic society. Those who manipulate this imperceptible social mechanism form an invisible government which really rules the country. [...] The techniques for regulating opinion were invented and developed as civilization became more complex and the need for invisible government more and more evident. [...] And if, according

to the established formula, such and such a presidential candidate
has been "designated" to respond to "an immense popular expecta-
tion", no one is unaware that in reality his name has been chosen by a
dozen gentlemen gathered in a small committee.[25]

How do you get someone to do something and make them feel
that they have freely chosen to do it? How to make the transgression
of the mental integrity of the popular masses remain unnoticed? How
can we make sure that the steering of the masses has all the appearances of democracy and respect for the sovereignty of the people? In
short, how do you rape someone without them noticing? These are
the questions of social *hacking* that the ruling elites ask themselves.
The journalist Sylvie Pierre-Brossolette, today head of the High
Council for Equality between Women and Men (HCE), declared on
January 16, 2008 on *France Info* about the European Union: "Don't
we have to rape the people a little bit for their own good? We do it
for other issues. [The abolition of the death penalty was voted for
behind the backs of the people, they did not want it. Europe is a bit
like that. A few months later, in the *Bibliothèque Médicis* program
of November 27, 2008, Alain Minc made similar remarks on the
television channel Public Sénat. These repeated calls for the "rape
of the people" were described by Serge Tchakhotine in 1939 in his
famous book, *Le Viol des foules par la propagande politique*. The rape
is always that of the critical and rational intelligence, to the benefit
of the emotions and the primary affects. Tchakhotine distinguished
four primary impulses on which manipulation surfs: aggressiveness,
immediate material interest, sexual attraction in the broad sense, the
search for security and the norm. The most effective manipulation
will be that which best instrumentalizes these primary impulses by

---

25. Bernays (Edward), *Propaganda. Comment manipuler l'opinion en démocratie*, La
Découverte, 2007, p. 31, 33 and 50.

promising the fullest and quickest satisfaction. These four impulses can ultimately be reduced to two primordial affects: sex and fear. The skilful use of these two affects, the alternate play on the carrot and the stick, seduction and anxiety, allows to lead a group by the nose, to pilot its change with its consent, thus to make imperceptible the rape of its own mental and political sovereignty.

The game on these two affects can, in its turn, be summarized to a single psychic motion, of phantasmatic and regressive type. Indeed, the techniques of influence to make something desirable, to make "sexy and glamorous" anything, are those of the advertising communication. However, all the staging of communication, marketing and advertising seduction are only the infinite declensions of one and the same original mental motion, which in psychoanalytical terms would be called the "elementary structure of the fantasy", that is to say the desire of fusion of oneself and others in an indistinct unity abolishing contradiction or, in other words, the fantasy of return to the maternal belly. Also referred to as the "oceanic feeling" or the quest for the "fusional group", this is the primordial fantasy of pre-oedipal regression on which all other fantasies in a human life are based. The phantasmatic field being a powerful motor of action, whoever succeeds best in flattering the regressive tendencies of the human by promising him the return to the uterus, generally wins over the group. The culture of involution towards archaic stages of the psyche, with the prospect of a return to a fetal stage, is thus presented as the guiding thread of all globalized psychopolitical engineering.

Tittytainment

The architects of globalization have understood this perfectly well: to be truly effective, the manufacture of consent presupposes the abolition of all borders. Indeed, it is the maintenance of borders, at all levels of existence, that makes comparison, contradiction, the possibility of saying "no" and the whole game of political dialectics that follows possible. It is also the maintenance of borders that supports economic protectionism, which is necessary if one wishes to preserve the material autonomy and intellectual independence that it allows. On the other hand, globalist engineering seeks as its ultimate goal to elaborate this famous "global village" without borders, which would provide the means to obtain the definitive consent of populations on all subjects, so as not to be forced to work on them constantly. With the abolition of borders, that is to say of the very principle of any exteriority, the possibility of any comparison and fundamental contradiction is also abolished, thus of any critical counter-power and any resistance. A globalized, unipolar world, without borders and politically unified under a centralized government and a single system of values and norms would put an end once and for all to the very possibility of thinking "differently". One world, one thought. In this respect, the engineering of the *Great Reset,* as the erasure of borders under a unique tutelage, is identified with a process of pre-Oedipal regression and deliberate infantilization of populations.

From the point of view of psychogenesis, the maternal bosom is experienced by the child as a continuity of its intra-uterine experience, that is to say as this unique and encompassing world, without exteriority, without limits, without borders, an absolute world, without comparison, relativization, or contradiction; and childhood is that age of life without politics, marked by the spontaneous adhesion to the dominant values of the social body, the conformist and gregarious immersion in the norms of the surrounding world, and especially the impotence to react against an alteration of its living conditions. To build the depoliticization of humanity, to build the "yes" to everything, the global consent, passes therefore by a provoked lowering of its average psychic maturity and its return in a kind of maternal lap extended to the whole world.

In order to build this general docility, Zbigniew Brzezinski, the famous advisor to American presidents who oversaw the creation of al-Qaeda in Afghanistan in the 1980s, proposed the concept of *Tittytainment*.[26] Two German journalists report on the birth of this concept at the first international State of the World Forum, held in September 1995 in a large Californian hotel: "The Fairmont Hotel in San Francisco is an ideal setting for dreams of global dimensions. [...] The future, the Fairmont pragmatists summarize in a fraction and a concept: "two-tenths" and "*tittytainment*". In the coming century, two-tenths of the working population would be enough to keep the world economy going. [But what about the rest? Can we envisage 80% of people who want to work being unemployed? "It is certain," says American author Jeremy Rifkin, who wrote the book *The End of Work*, "that the other 80 percent will have considerable problems." [...] It is a new social order that is being drawn in Fairmont, a world of rich countries, without a middle class worthy of the name - and nobody is denying it. The expression "*tittytainment*", proposed by that old grunt Zbigniew Brzezinski, is on the other hand making a career. The Polish-born Brzezinski spent four years as National Security Advisor to US President Jimmy Carter. Since then, he has devoted himself

---

26. JAUVERT (Vincent) (interview with), "Oui, la CIA est entrée en Afghanistan avant les Russes...", *Le Nouvel Observateur*, 15 January 1998: http://hebdo.nouvelobs.com/hebdo/parution/p19980115/articles/a19460-.html

Governing by chaos

to geostrategic issues. *Tittytainment,* according to Brzezinski, is a combination of the words *entertainment* and *tits*, the American slang term for breasts. Brzezinski is thinking less of sex, in this case, than of the milk that flows from a nursing mother's breast. A cocktail of mind-numbing entertainment and sufficient food would, according to him, keep the world's frustrated population in a good mood. [...] We are seeing the emergence of the two-tenths society, the one where we will have to resort to *tittytainment* to keep the excluded quiet."[27]

Proponents of the Great Reinitialization come to the same conclusion: with artificial intelligence, automation and robotization of work, 80% of the population will become useless. Several avenues are being considered to manage and reduce this obsolete human mass. With its *Project Coast* program led by Dr. Wouter Basson, the apartheid regime in South Africa was a pioneer in the development of biological weapons injected in the form of vaccines to sterilize and eventually eliminate certain categories of the population. The military-industrial complex of many countries, as well as the WHO and various actors such as Bill Gates' Gavi Foundation for Vaccines, naturally looked into this research. The mortality rates and serious side effects of Covid-19 vaccines argue for malicious intent on the part of the manufacturers. The residual human biomass that escaped the hecatomb could be managed by non-authoritarian social control based on universal income, *tittytainment* and digital alienation in cyberspace (metaverses) via avatars. The hollow and infantilizing dream in which Brzezinski proposes to enclose the populations in order to better control them has the characteristics of a kind of completely depoliticized virtual reality, a global Disneyland based on consumption and the Spectacle. The total securitization of the power of the elites

---

27. MARTIN (Hans-Peter) and SCHUMANN (Harald), *Le Piège de la mondialisation*, Actes Sud, 1997, p. 13-20.

necessarily relies on the derealization of the existence of the plebs, a derealization that consists of a relentless "re-enchantment of the world" (theme of the MEDEF's 2005 summer university), the aim of which is to get someone to dig his own grave gently, then to lower him down with a smile and cover himself with earth in a joyful and good mood. One will recognize here the sociological tendency known as the *cocooning*, playing the role of a new opium of the people, much more effective than the religion, because completely devoid of effect of sublimation. Social engineering thus aims at making tolerable, and even desirable, a profoundly morbid civilizational involution by adorning it with all the features of perpetual rejuvenation, thus apparently with vitality and future, with, as its ultimate goal, the "fetalization" of humanity by means of its insertion into a social environment conceived in the image of an immense artificial womb, that is to say, devoid of borders and contradictions. The intra-uterine stage and, by extension, all the immature stages (newborns, infants, babies and young children) are characterized, certainly by their organic vitality, but especially by their easily malleable mental plasticity as well as their state of total alienation, completely at the mercy of others (the Freudian *Hilflosigkeit*).

It is thus a question of reproducing in the extra-uterine the conditions of an intra-uterine existence: fusion with others in a great homogeneous and enveloping whole, obedience to the general movement, continuous and immediate enjoyment, completeness, unified identity, absence of tensions, contradictions, contestations, pure positivity, thus end of History, end of all, in a word, paradise, the definitive cocoon! Numerous authors have critically studied the aspects of this globalized pre-Oedipal regression, starting with Gilles Châtelet in his *Vivre et penser comme des porcs. De l'incitation à l'envie et à l'ennui dans les démocraties-marchés.* Other titles are no less eloquent, from Jean-Claude Michéa, *L'Enseignement de l'ignorance et ses conditions modernes*, to Dany-Robert Dufour, *L'Art de réduire les têtes. On the new servitude of the liberated man in the era of total capitalism*, through Charles Melman and Jean-Pierre Lebrun, *L'Homme sans gravité. Jouir à tout prix*, Michel Schneider, *Big Mother. Psychopathology of Political Life*, and Jean-Claude Liaudet, *Le Complexe d'Ubu ou la Névrose libérale*. All these texts are devoted to the analysis of contemporary social control in its unprecedented specificities, namely the depoliticization of the masses through the establishment of a type of society based on the characteristics of the maternal womb, inducing a lowering of the average mental age as well as a certain number of new mental pathologies revolving around depression and perversion. By seeking to abolish all borders, and therefore all limits, and in the same gesture the very notion of exteriority, of the external, objective, real world, globalist engineering thus seeks to build a form of derealized society based on a culture of interiority, of the carnal fusion in a homogeneous identity block and of the correlative rejection of all that is heterogeneous, other, in short of all that reminds the Father, that is to say the authority that cracks the exclusive and encompassing hold of the maternal world to introduce to the "external world" and to the real.

Foot-in-the-door

Another way of constructing consent to regression is based on what could be called "engineering of the obliging situation". In their classic work on social psychology, *Petit traité de manipulation à l'usage des honnêtes gens*, the two researchers Robert-Vincent Joule and Jean-Léon Beauvois describe several behavioural induction strategies which, each time, respect the feeling of freedom of the manipulated subjects. In all cases, it is a matter of constructing "voluntary servitude", that is to say, making the manipulated subject not only accept, but also desire what has, in fact, been decided in his place, by putting him in a situation of commitment to pursue a behavior. The foot-in-the-door technique, or "sausage technique", which consists in making the subject swallow the whole thing in small slices, is one of the best known. Joule and Beauvois summarize it as follows: "[...] a non-problematic and inexpensive preparatory behavior is extorted from the subject [...] Once this preparatory behavior has been obtained, a request is explicitly addressed to the subject inviting him or her to perform a new behavior, this time more costly and one that he or she was unlikely to perform spontaneously."[28] By proceeding in a gradual manner, it is thus possible to gradually orient the approach of a subject (individual or group) and even to make him undertake "freely" a deterioration of his situation, while giving him the impression that he is improving his lot and that he is acting of his own accord, whereas he has been made to make an irrational decision that goes against his interest.

The psychological study of the induction of irrational decision-making was initiated by Lewin in his famous behavioral modification experiments, which Joule and Beauvois briefly recall: "We must be grateful to Kurt Lewin (1947) for having first insisted on such consequences of decision-making activity. There is no need to recall in detail these now famous experiments in which he compares the effectiveness of two strategies aimed at modifying the consumption habits of American housewives (buying low cuts of butcher's meat rather

---

28. JOULE (Robert-Vincent) and BEAUVOIS (Jean-Léon), *Petit traité de manipulation à l'usage des honnêtes gens,* Presses universitaires de Grenoble, 2002, p. 103.

than noble cuts, powdered milk rather than fresh milk, etc.)".[29] This factory of consent to change directed "downwards" always requires a lot of delicacy in the way of proceeding. Any precipitation or massive attack is forbidden. Thus, as early as 1996, a report published in the *Economic Policy Brief of the* Organisation for Economic Co-operation and Development (OECD) made the following recommendations for liquidating state public services with the least possible reaction: "If operating expenses are reduced, care must be taken not to reduce the *quantity of* service, even if this means that the *quality of the service will* decline. For example, you can cut operating funds to schools or universities, but it would be dangerous to cut the number of students. Families will react violently to a refusal to enrol their children, but not to a gradual decline in the quality of education, and the school can gradually and punctually obtain a contribution from families, or eliminate a particular activity. This is done piecemeal, in one school, but not in the neighboring school, so that general public discontent is avoided."[30]

Obtaining unproblematic consent to degradation can also be considerably facilitated by a starting situation that is, or at least is perceived to be, problematic. Since every human situation is in some way problematic, it is only necessary to accentuate certain aspects of it, to blacken the picture in order to demand saving "reforms". If necessary, the problem is created by internal sabotage, in the form of a reduction in operating budgets, a cleverly inflated public debt (by taking interest into account in the overall calculation), or any form of planned crisis, economic, diplomatic, social, etc. Then a solution is

---

29. *Op. cit.* p. 30.
30. Morrisson (Christian), "The Feasibility of Adjustment," in *Economic Policy Brief* No. 13, OECD Development Centre, 1996, p. 30: http://www.cip-idf.org/IMG/pdf/ocde_n_13_.pdf

proposed. This proposed solution will only make things worse, but since it is the only path to change suggested to the group, they have the impression of an improvement by simply changing their position. The simple fact of changing something produces the impression of changing for the better, because the human psyche is so made that it always envisages positively at the beginning the exit of a difficult situation. This cognitive reflex is the consequence of an instinctive optimism, of biological origin, without which the living being could not maintain itself in life. This infatuation lasts only until we realize that it was only to go to worse. And then another solution is immediately proposed, which in turn will only make the situation worse, but which will be received temporarily with enthusiasm, and so on ad infinitum without it ever being possible to go back to the origin of the problem to really solve it, because one finds oneself continually deported further and further from its roots. Change management thus aims to implant in people's minds a systematic "It was worse before", prohibiting any conservatism or backtracking, whatever the situation, even the most degraded, that one experiences. It is a matter of inducing a forced forward march from point A to point B, by programming a kind of blind hope and obtuse optimism for point B, presented as necessarily better than point A, backward-looking and reactionary, the whole based on a good dose of autosuggestion, historical revisionism and ideological progressism.

Mind Control

Let's take another step in the provoked mental regression and social piracy. Everyone remembers the words of Patrick Le Lay, then chairman and CEO of TF1, about the "available brain time" that his television channel was selling to advertisers. There is nothing anecdotal in this formulation. After the control of emotions and situations, social engineering has been very interested in the direct control of the brain, with the aim of short-circuiting the field of representations in order to directly attack the programming of the nervous system in its most raw materiality. This analogy between brain and computer, already perceptible in cybernetics, cognitivism and *social learning*, is in fact based on *learning in the* strict sense of teaching a living being to behave in a certain way. To put it bluntly, *learning* is the science of training and behavioral conditioning. It was originally tested on laboratory animals, but was quickly applied to humans in the 1940s through research into *Mind Control*, or MK (*Mind Kontrol*), carried out with the aim of creating "Manchurian candidates" and perfect soldiers, who would ignore fear, be insensitive to pain, etc. Various protocols were developed, which were based on the principle of "learning". Various protocols were developed, based on the behaviourist principles of "classical conditioning", derived from Pavlov's work on conditioned reflexes (direct and deterministic strategy) and "operant conditioning", derived from Skinner's work on the induction of behaviours from the shaping of the environment (indirect and tendentious strategy).

As the game of reward and punishment can go as far as torture, it is not surprising that the American MK-Ultra research program, whose files were recently declassified after having been top-secret for some fifty years, has strongly inspired not only the aforementioned book by Naomi Klein, but also Gordon Thomas's very thorough investigation, entitled *The CIA's Secret Weapons. Torture, manipulation and chemical weapons*. The author gives a complete history of the MK-Ultra project, with its mad scientists busy with their human guinea pigs, or "disposable subjects", as they put it. The Germanization of the term *control* into *Kontrolle* was a nod to the origins of the scientists who first developed this research, former Nazis exfiltrated after the war to the United States or England under Operation Paperclip. Thus, since 1945, and in the continuity of what the scientists of the Third Reich had begun to develop, numerous experiments on hypnosis, hallucinogens, subliminal influence, brainwashing and mental reprogramming were (and continue to be) elaborated on individuals and on the masses at the Massachusetts Institute of Technology (MIT), at the Tavistock Institute or on other university campuses such as Harvard. The unfortunate Ted Kaczynski, who became famous under the pseudonym Unabomber, was himself a victim in the early 1960s, while still a student under Henry A. Murray. More recently, a new discipline, neuromarketing, has emerged from this research, based on medical imaging of the brain and explicitly aiming at triggering irrepressible buying impulses by the targeted activation of certain areas of the nervous system.

Mind Control is fond of computer and artificial intelligence metaphors, its project consisting in rewriting the behavioral program of a living machine, but without this machine realizing it. Psychosociobiological hacking, where the source code of the subject has been cracked, then erased and reformatted by an entity external to the subject, which has thus become the owner of the subject's unconscious and which can therefore direct its future. A *hacker* has infiltrated the memory, taken control of it, reconfigured it according to his plans, implemented new *habitus*, new behavioral algorithms and now pilots the human machine remotely. But above all, he has erased all traces of his break-in and manipulation. The philosophy of *Mind Control*, the total control over a living being, a control authorized by the reduction of this being to a computational machine simply animated by *inputs* and *outputs* of information, has thus infused all modern politics, progressively reduced to the management of quantitative flows. Cybernetics, even when it claims to be "humanistic" in the conferences of the Macy Foundation (1946-1953) or in the Meadows Report of the Club of Rome (1972), cannot help but seek to reduce uncertainty to zero and thus to produce a chosification of the living being.

These various approaches to the management of human groups all have in common that they produce a levelling down effect. Each time, it is a question of bypassing the frontal lobe of the brain, the neocortex, seat of language and dialectical functions, to take direct control of the pre-linguistic functions: the primitive reflexes of the reptilian brain, and the emotions in the limbic system. It is a question of making sublimation impossible, that is to say of desiring words rather than objects, and of maintaining all life between two simplified pre-language mental states, derived from the two primitive emotions which are fear and erogenous excitation. This atrophy of the psychic field obviously generates a whole range of depressive states and diverse mental pathologies, which we can gather under the terms of desymbolization, loss of meaning and mental structure. But, in order to achieve its ends, i.e. the construction of a totally safe and predictable social system, the political engineering of the developed countries has had no other choice than to consider the human being as less than an animal: as a simple plastic object, available to be recomposed at will.

Virtualism

This plasticity allows all transgressions and rewritings of reality. In political engineering, when the real behavior of a population, for example at the time of a vote, does not correspond to the predictions of the authorities, a virtual smoothing comes to rewrite and correct this reality to adjust it to the prediction. This smoothing can take several forms. The most brutal consists in pretending that nothing has happened and in ignoring the results of the vote. People say "no" to a referendum, but we pretend they said "yes. Unfortunately, such an enormous distortion of the facts reveals the true nature of the power in place. A piece of reality appears, the virtualization is not perfect. It is obviously more subtle to hide the rigging of the results in legal procedures, as was the case for the 2000 presidential elections in the United States. In the future, the dematerialization of voting, the replacement of ballot boxes and ballots with digital bits and electronic voting will greatly facilitate the systematic rigging of elections and the unabashed rewriting of reality. As a warning, studies conducted by Chantal Enguehard, a researcher in computer science at the Centre national de la recherche scientifique (CNRS), have already revealed the falsifications introduced by voting machines in the presidential, legislative and municipal elections of 2007 and 2008 in France.[31]

The rewriting of a reality that does not fit the forecasts is part of this fantasy of predictability and absolute reduction of uncertainty, a fantasy of maximum security of the system that characterizes politics when it is under "scientific" influence. If this security fantasy seems legitimate in the scientific field, it induces collateral effects in the socio-political field that can be summarized as follows: aspiration to a total control of the real, thus general reification, chosification, transformation of subjects into objects and of the living into non-living. The real being, according to Jacques Lacan's topological and structural definition, "that which cannot be controlled", social engineering

---

31. "Une étude pointe les failles du vote électronique", *Le Nouvel Observateur*, July 8, 2008: http://tempsreel.nouvelobs.com/actualites/politique/20080708.OBS2090/une_etude_pointe_les_failles_du_vote_electronique.html

aims neither more nor less than to abolish the real. In favor of what? In favor of a perfectly controlled derealization, what Jean Baudrillard called a "simulacrum" (or a "simulation"). In topological terms, the real is not a thing or a substance (no ontology), but a place, a position. Anything can be in the position of real, as soon as one stumbles upon it and does not control it. As such, even the virtual can be in the position of real, the "true" virtual not being the opposite of the real, but the abolition of the distinction between the two. The real is thus the other name of the original antagonism that founds our psychic lives, the fundamental contradiction of things that sets a limit to our will to power. In the political field, the real is thus everything that is in a position of counter-power. It is therefore also everything that poses a threat to the safety and security of my power, as I would like it to be central and exclusive.

The body of research initiated by Michel Foucault and Giorgio Agamben shows in detail how this security mutation of politics follows a prison logic. Since the reflection of political power is now limited to the means of totally securing the management of populations, criminology quite naturally becomes the new theoretical paradigm. As the ruling elites seek to abolish all counter-power and all contradiction, it goes without saying that permanent surveillance and the normative engineering of groups take precedence over the debate of contradictory ideas. This concentrationist drift of society, however, obeys a double standard. The French state is capable of treating simple political activists as "S" terrorists on the grounds that they have traveled to Russia, and at the same time of repatriating Islamic State (Daech) jihadists and their children on the grounds that they are of French origin. The annihilation of any contradiction, or better, the staging of pseudo-contradictions, pseudo-power struggles and pseudo-alternations that give the impression of saving the political real, but emptying it of all its substance, this securing of the political field by fiction is the exclusive goal pursued by our modern advisors to the Prince, political consultants, *spin doctors* and great architects of the social body who spend their time orienting the perception of the real and building pyramid-like group structures, of which they will be the "all-seeing eye" at the top. The strategic analysis journal *De defensa* has called this state of "virtualism", in which the perception of the political field is voluntarily disconnected from reality.[32] The contemporary reign of pseudo-antagonisms, with the outward signs of contradiction, but whose polarities apparently engaged in a power struggle are in reality in collusion or under the control of the floor above, is thus bringing us into the era of security virtualization and the abolition of reality in politics.

Counter-insurgency warfare

In their work of virtualization of the political field, the social engineers have been inspired by the methods of counter-insurgency warfare. Manufacturing the consent of the people requires knowing how to circumvent, neutralize, and annihilate the risks of revolt on their part. Faced with the various insurrections that have marked the 20th century, decolonization wars, revolutions, guerrilla wars, uprisings and social conflicts that destabilize power, military officers in various countries have sought to formalize counterinsurgency tactics, in other words, techniques for the successful repression of any form of popular resistance to power, if possible

32. GRASSET (Philippe), "Le virtualisme est désormais identifié à Washington : faith-based community contre reality-based community", October 23, 2004: http://www.dedefensa.org/article.php?art_id=1250

nipping protest in the bud even before it appears. The best known manuals are those of Roger Trinquier, *La Guerre moderne* (1961), David Galula, *Contre-insurrection. Theory and Practice* (1964-2008) and Frank Kitson, *Low Intensity Operations. Subversion, Insurgency and Peacekeeping* (1971).

British General Frank Kitson (b. 1926) has held the highest offices and decorations, including *Commander in Chief, Land Command* of the Royal Army from 1982 to 1985, General Aide-de-Camp to Queen Elizabeth II from 1983 to 1985, and Knight Grand Cross of the Order of the British Empire. With years of experience in the field and numerous feats of arms (Kenya, Malaysia, Northern Ireland, Falklands), he has written a manual in which he summarizes the methods to be used by an army corps seeking to impose itself on a local population that resists it. This book, with its confidential edition, has never been translated into French and we know of only five copies in French university libraries (see the Sudoc catalog). In fact, the dissemination of this text to a large audience could single-handedly tip over entire geopolitical balances. The investigative journalist Michel Collon sums up the content of this Grail of political thought as follows: "General though he is, Kitson considers that classic military and police repression has no chance of succeeding without a 'campaign to win hearts and minds', which he calls 'strategic psychological warfare'. What does this mysterious term mean? It becomes clearer when we examine all the methods Kitson advocates and uses: - Training all the important executives of the ministries (Army, Foreign Affairs...) in "psy ops" techniques (psychological manipulation of opinion). - Set up "pseudogangs" that will gather a maximum of information. But above all, by carrying out "coups" attributed to the enemy, they will discredit him. - Use the "special forces" (SAS) to carry out attacks that will be attributed to the enemy in order to increase tension and justify repression. - Create diversions, for example by provoking a "war of religion". - Fabricate false documents ("black propaganda") that will be attributed to the enemy in order to discredit him. - Infiltrate agents, or recruit traitors (by blackmail or corruption), within the opponent's organizations in order to discredit him, or even to provoke splits. - Militarize the BBC news and totally censor the opposing point of view. To filter information to the international press, and to ensure complicity. Provide photographic material to influence opinion. Using journalists as spies in the field. - Using music to attract young people with an apparently "depoliticized" message. - Setting up and popularizing fake "spontaneous" movements, presented as neutral and independent, in reality financed and controlled in order to divide and weaken support for the opposing side." [33]

Kitson reviews the entire arsenal of current politics: the creation of false enemies, false friends, false problems and false solutions by means of false perceptions induced by false terrorist attacks (known as *false flags* or "under a false banner" in military jargon) and false information (black propaganda, entirely false, or grey, a mixture of true and false to better convey the false), all of which can be summed up under the abbreviation psy ops, for "psychological operations". Fake mass graves in Romania, Yugoslavia, Ukraine, fake weapons of mass destruction in Iraq, real chemical attacks but false testimonies to accuse the government in Syria or elsewhere, *Fake News are* becoming the norm and form the enveloping backdrop of the global environment, with its catastrophic consequences on the individual psyche. In his 1978 Harvard speech, Alexander Solzhenitsyn denounced the empire of lies embodied by the liberal West that he discovered as a Soviet dissident. However, it is only a question of

---

33. GOLINGER (Eva), *Code Chavez. CIA contre Venezuela*, preface by Michel Collon, Oser Dire, 2006, p. 24.

Governing by chaos

dosage. In the society of the Spectacle, the true is only a moment of the false. But, as Christian Harbulot and his co-editors point out in *La Guerre cognitive*, lies, manipulation, deception and trickery are the immemorial tools of politics, as a mental war of images, words and representations for the control of minds. In the very first chapter of his classic textbook, Sun Tzu wrote, "The whole art of war is based on deception." More recently, General Francart explains in great detail in *The War of Meaning*, subtitled *Why and How to Act in Psychological Fields*, how propaganda must be inspired by the methods of advertising communication to obtain the consent, or even the favor, of the targeted populations. And, indeed, it is in the 20th century that the derealization of the political field reached its apogee thanks to the mass media, in particular the television, marvellous tool of social control, spy infiltrated until the rooms of the teenagers, which came to shape the perceptions and to form the vision of the world of millions of citizens. Television, the main vector of psy ops, has allowed and still allows whole populations to enter a virtual reality entirely constructed by the power.

Reality-building

Reality-building, the science of constructing reality, has no official existence as a theory or constituted practice. But, a bit like those cosmic singularities that are black holes, it is possible to infer its existence from the effects it produces. Christian Salmon's analyses in *Storytelling - La machine à fabriquer des histoires et à formater les esprits* (2007) put us on the track. Indeed, *storytelling*, a theory in vogue among political, management and marketing consultants, already fully assumes that *leadership* and group management are based on "storytelling". The stories we tell can be based on reality, on objective facts, but not necessarily. Here, truth and real facts are secondary. *Storytelling* is essentially based on the elaboration of a good narrative, which can be a good fiction, exciting or anxiety-provoking, and which applies narrative schemes and scenaristic structures that have already proved their worth in literature or cinema. The imagery and the spectacular stagings aim at making people dream and at producing on demand this or that type of emotion in the public, in order to ensure the predictability of its behavior and to keep the system under control. Not to respond to the reactions of the people, but to create them outright, in order to be always one step ahead of them. This is the objective of Klaus Schwab and Thierry Malleret, two pillars of the "Davos Forum", in *The Grand Narrative - For a Better Future*, published in 2022 as a sequel to *Covid-19: The Great Reinitialization*: "Narratives provide the context in which the facts we observe can be interpreted, understood and exploited. In this sense, they represent much more than the stories we tell, write, or figuratively illustrate; they end up being the truths, or the ideas we accept as truths, that underlie the perceptions that shape our "realities" and, in so doing, form our cultures and societies. Through narratives, we explain how we see things, how they work, how we make decisions and justify them, how we understand our place in the world, and how we try to persuade others to adhere to our beliefs and values. In short, stories shape our perceptions, which in turn shape our realities and ultimately influence our choices and actions. This is how we find meaning in life. This book offers a constellation of interrelated narratives that shed light on what is to come and what is to be done. The Grand Narrative is built around a central story and is the result of a collaborative effort with some of the world's leading thinkers. It aims to shape longer-term perspectives and co-create a narrative that can help create a more resilient, inclusive, and sustainable vision for our collective future."[34]

In this constructivist approach, we can pose the equation: narrative = reality. In fact, we only have access to reality through the prism of language. This filter is sometimes distorting. In any case, it has a certain plasticity. Language allows us to pixelate reality - by pixelating the image of reality - and then to break it down, point by point, to reconstruct it according to a new plan. Since 2020 and the launch of the *Great Reset* at Covid-19, Schwab and Malleret have been working to dissolve the human condition and the infinite multitude of narratives and realities that comprise it to recoagulate them into the Great Narrative, singular, that will shape the new, unique post-human global reality, the one defined by Schwab, Malleret and their associates. Before unifying the world under a single governance, and managing the whole planet from a wall of screens in an office in Geneva, a single narrative for all humanity must be defined and accepted, a single software that will allow the world machine to be reinitialized on the basis of a single program, a single discourse, allowing the harmonization of the functioning of all brains. Like all great utopians, Klaus Schwab is a pacifist. The search for consensus, that is, the reduction of the multiple and of antagonisms, has been Schwab's fixed idea since he created the World Economic Forum in 1971, whether through his concept of "stakeholder capitalism" or in geopolitics. The anguish of Schwab, and of globalists in general, is the fragmentation of the world, which he deplored at the G20 meeting in 2022, particularly because of the war in Ukraine, a multipolar fragmentation that must be abolished and restructured into a central Grand Narrative and a single unipolar global reality. This utopian

---

34. SCHWAB (Klaus) and MALLERET (Thierry), *The Grand Narrative - For a Better Future*, 2022, Forum Publishing, p. 14.

fantasy of building a unified and pacified world reality through the elaboration of a single collective narrative for all humanity is only possible through the elimination of all diversity, otherness, exteriority, which is the very mechanism of psychosis and the invasion of fiction, when the limit between oneself and the other wavers and one no longer distinguishes between subjective representations and the external world. The single Great World Narrative is therefore above all the Great Fiction.

Undoubtedly reinforced by the progress of audiovisual and computer technologies, it seems that political marketing makes an ever increasing use of fiction. In this sense, *reality-building*, which aims to take the greatest possible liberty with regard to reality, is nothing more than the radicalized, uninhibited concept of propaganda and *story-telling*: we are no longer satisfied with telling a story, we plan to make others enter completely into a virtual reality that we have constructed from A to Z. Political journalist Ron Suskind reported in 2004 on a conversation he once had with an adviser to George W. Bush: "In the summer of 2002, after I wrote an article in *Esquire* that the White House didn't like about former Bush communications director Karen Hughes, I had a discussion with a senior Bush adviser. He expressed the White House's displeasure to me, and then he told me something that I didn't fully understand at the time - but which I now believe goes to the very heart of the Bush presidency. The adviser told me that guys like me were "in what we call the reality-based community," which he defined as people who "believe that solutions emerge from the judicious study of discernible reality." I nodded, and muttered something about the principles of reason and empiricism. He cut me off. "That's not the way the world works anymore," he continued. "We are now an empire, and when we act, we create our own reality. And as you study that reality - judiciously, no doubt - we will act again, creating other new realities, which you can study as well, and that's how things will work out. We are the actors of history... and you, all of you, will just have to study what we do."[35]

The uneasiness caused by these remarks comes from the fact that we are witnessing the unabashed transgression of a taboo. Something sacred is trampled under our eyes. And indeed, *reality-building* does not hesitate to transgress the fundamental law of the human condition, the ultimate law of our lives, that is to say the confrontation with reality, the fact that there is always something "that cannot be controlled". Everyone, whatever his position in the social hierarchy, must submit to this arbitrator, to this fundamental and founding authority that, by definition, no one controls and that therefore remains totally impartial and incorruptible. We are all equal in front of reality. But social engineering aims precisely at escaping this common human condition in order to elaborate an unequal form of life and politics, where the top of the pyramid would be completely detached from the base, where the fantasy of the dominant would take the place of reality to become the exclusive Law of the dominated. This old dream of putting one's own desire in the place of reality, the dream of being able to realize all our fantasies, to abolish all limits and all that resists our desire, is itself an effect of our condition as humans, all too human, for whom the perception of reality is always decoupled from reality itself. Homo sapiens is indeed not in direct contact with the real. His relationship to reality is always mediated by a perceptual construction, a representation, which we call reality. As Alfred Korzybski thematized in his General

---

35. SUSKIND (Ron), "Without a Doubt. Faith, Certainty, and the Presidency of George W. Bush," *New York Times*, October 17, 2004: http://www.nytimes.com/2004/10/17/magazine/17BUSH.html?ex=1255665600&en=890a96189e162076&ei=5090&partner=rssuserland

Semantics, the relationship between reality and its representation is exactly on the model of the territory and its map. Certainly, we live in a real territory, but we need to internalize a map of this territory, thus a representation of this real, to survive in it. The construction of the map is done by means of signs. But the arbitrariness of the sign, highlighted by Ferdinand de Saussure, the fact that signs have no natural relation with what they designate, obliges any construction of meaning to be conventional, therefore cultural, historical, relative and negotiable. The human being thus lives in a paradox, with one foot in a plastic and constructible reality, a semantic representation of a real, uncontrollable, uncontrollable and asemantic where he puts the other foot.

If we cannot construct reality directly, we can therefore try to approach it asymptotically by constructing a reality. Then, the widely shared mechanism of the self-fulfilling prophecy does the rest: by dint of acting and thinking according to a certain image of reality, we come to shape reality itself according to this image. It is the various means of achieving this that constructivist theory has analyzed, notably in the collective work *The Invention of Reality*, from the Palo Alto school, of which Paul Watzlawick is the best known member. From constructivism, many strategic applications have been drawn, aimed at eliminating all forms of contestation. Thus, a technique applied in the corporate world, the "multiplied message", consists in orchestrating through internal memos the circulation of the same information with small variations and through different channels to elaborate an apparently decentralized and uncoordinated informational landscape, a reality resembling the real, but fundamentally univocal and consensual, from which the real has in fact been evacuated. At the very least, if there is actual disagreement in the group, or even declared conflict, that is fine, but it must not be perceived in any way.

Other techniques of *reality-building* are based on the systematic inversion of the meaning of words and the elaboration of contradictory syntagms in the terms, paralyzing the critical reflection. This activity of linguistic construction of a non-polemical reality, a purely positive reality, from which all negativity has been evacuated, George Orwell had, in his time, baptized it the "novlanguage". Taking up the witness, Éric Hazan, in *LQR. La propagande du quotidien*, highlights the intentionally derealizing alterations that contemporary managerial power makes to language, which are on a par with those analyzed by Victor Klemperer in *LTI, la langue du IIIe Reich*. In the same spirit, Stuart Ewen reports this advice from advertising marketing: "To sell commercial culture, it was necessary to propose a vision of it purified of any cause of social discontent. [...] Helen Woodward, a leading authority on advertising copywriting in the 1920s, said that to write an effective ad the designer must religiously avoid the world of production. "Whatever product you have to advertise," she recommended, "never go to the place where it is made [...] Never watch people work [...] Because, you see, when you know the truth of anything, the real, deep truth, it becomes very difficult to compose the light, superficial prose that is going to sell that thing.""[36]

As we can see, marketing often relies on a good dose of doublethink, in the sense of Orwell, i.e. autosuggestion. The suggestion, and especially the autosuggestion, of a fictitious reality that enchants what is being promoted or that exaggeratedly denigrates an adversary, are part of the basic propaganda techniques common to totalitarian regimes and to "sales force" schools. In *The Falsifiers*, writer and company director Antoine Bello, founder of the multinational Ubiqus, describes a secret international organization,

---

36. EWEN (Stuart), *op. cit.* pp. 121-122.

the Consortium for the Falsification of Reality (CFR), whose work consists, under the cover of consulting firms, in rewriting and inventing entire episodes of world history. A work on the borderline between fiction and autobiography, illustrating once again the links between politics and management in the contemporary war on reality. In all cases, it is a question of enclosing subjectivity, oneself or others, in a mental construction with the dimensions of a complete virtual reality; but so that the illusion holds, the gesture of the intentional construction must be carefully dissimulated. It is necessary to manage to essentialize and naturalize the social and linguistic construction, however delusional it may be, to make it THE reality, unique and incontestable. What is fantasy for some then becomes law for others. In short, "Move along, nothing to see here".

All political marketing operations, the shaping of perceptions and the construction of reality have as their goal the abolition of reality, and therefore ultimately the depoliticization of the debate, by means of the establishment of a system of decoys and feints. The role of disinformation (intox and *deception*), which is also crucial in the military and intelligence fields, consists of capturing and distracting attention, diverting perceptions to false dangers in order to occupy available brain time with false alarms and send the enemy on false leads, for example by inventing terrorists and fabricating evidence, if necessary. On the political level, this device has only one goal, never to address the only serious question, the question that makes people angry, that is to say the class struggle, the wealth gaps between social classes, and the efforts to reduce these gaps. Identity-based communitarianism, originally located more on the right of the political spectrum, has migrated to the left under a new name: *wokism*. As an engineering of perceptions, this sleight of hand is based on the following method: in order to blur the perception of the big politically troublesome differences, i.e. the differences of capital, ethnic, religious, gender, sexual orientation differences are dramatized, emphasized, exacerbated so that they occupy the whole field of perception and attention. The big real differences remain, but well camouflaged, possibly mixed with others, and therefore diluted and more difficult to grasp. By accentuating the secondary differences on the political level, *wokism* also makes it possible to break down the solidarities within the middle and working classes, to divide the poor between them, to set them against each other in order to weaken them.

Negative management

Divide and conquer. As a weapon of massive cognitive destruction, communitarianism introduces into a given population a plurality of cultural codes that break its lines of communication, a prerequisite for its tactical disorganization. Favoring heterogeneity and individualization of codes, atomizing, segmenting and breaking the lines of transmission, leading to the rupture of the coordination of the parties and the impossibility of organizing. Within the human species, everything is based on the organization of groups. The individual is only an abstraction, only the groups exist: the family, the village, the clan, the tribe, the friends, the colleagues, the social class, the party, the union, the nation, the ethnic group, the co-religionists, the species as a whole, etc. Homo sapiens only lives in groups, he is intrinsically gregarious, he is a "political animal", as Aristotle noted. Management is the science of the conscious organization of groups, i.e. the political gesture in its purest form, which even precedes the debate on ideas. But once we know the deep dynamics of group organization, we also know the deep dynamics of group disorganization. Based on the discoveries of social psychology, in particular game theory, management has become very interested in the detailed dissection of the mechanisms of decision making and the phenomena of commitment to action. A good manager, a good *leader* obviously knows how to galvanize his troops and push them to effective action, but he also knows how to inhibit decision making and commitment to action, and therefore how to paralyze an enemy group, as a prelude to its dislocation, and then to its disappearance. The hidden part of management and politics, the somewhat shameful part, because frankly Machiavellian, is therefore the art of disorganizing groups, the art of atomizing, splitting up, fragmenting collectives, therefore the art of instilling individualism. This "black mass", which can be guessed between the lines in classic management courses, is on the other hand totally explained in private and confidential seminars, reserved for the best placed executives of power structures, in particular in intelligence (economic intelligence, industrial, military, diplomatic espionage, etc.).

Management is therefore the art of organizing "friendly groups" - positive management - and the art of disorganizing "enemy groups" - negative management. In politics, the mastery of this art is more important than the ideas themselves and the debate on these ideas. For, in fact, the infrastructure of ideas is the organizational capacity of the human groups that support them. To make the expression of such an idea impossible without ever explicitly censoring it, it is enough to disorganize the group that supports it. Indirect censorship, by disorganization, discouragement, demotivation of the group, is a strategy of circumvention that has proven itself. The Cointelpro program, developed from 1956 onwards by American intelligence to fight against "internal enemies", was based almost entirely on this art of provoked decohesion. A group that is dislocated or simply unable to organize itself is no longer able to support this idea or that value. Even before arguing about ideas and values, we must therefore already reflect on the capacity to support, propagate and disseminate ideas, values and representations. In other words, the debate on the organization of the group precedes the debate on the ideas to defend. Who knows how to organize and disorganize human groups holds the supreme power. Because he holds the power to make ideas exist or not. Thus the power to produce or to extinguish behaviors. The social architecture commands the ideas, which command the behaviors, which build the reality.

Before analyzing negative management more precisely, let's present the fundamentals of positive management. A group is a set. For Lacan, human groups can be understood in terms of the logic of sets, or the mathematical theory of sets. Lacan distinguishes at least four modes of organization, relational modes that he calls discourses: the discourse of the master, where the leader dominates; the discourse of the hysteric, where the individual dominates; the academic discourse, where knowledge dominates; and the analytic discourse, where uncertainty dominates. (Lacan also mentions a fifth discourse once in his work, that of the capitalist, which seems to us to be a variant of the discourse of the hysteric.) The formation of a human ensemble, thus the organization of a group, requires the submission of individuals to a vertical hierarchy, to a discourse of the master, an authority, a Law, a symbolic phallus in a position of exception with respect to the members of the group. This relation of all the individuals to a transcendent authority is the only way for the individuals of this group to perceive themselves as unified before being individuals, thus as members of a single organism, a *sine qua non* condition to ensure their systemic cohesion, their solidarity and their efficiency in action. This is how their multitude will be coordinated and how they will act "as one". At the risk of a play on words, organizing a group always means basing it on values that we gather under the term "virility": structure, discipline, supervision, authority, cohesion and solidarity. In fact, for thousands of years, the male passion has always been to organize groups, whether for better or for worse, the organizational phenomenon having no intrinsic content. What Lacan calls being "all phallic" is recognizing oneself in a whole, a community that is bigger than us and to which we are ready to sacrifice our individual lives, because we do not exist outside of it. From this point of view, there is no enjoyment in being other than collective, there is no meaning to life other than in common, which makes the individual capable of fighting to the death to defend the ideas of his reference group. "The values of my group deserve that I can fight until death for them, the life of the group passes before mine", such is the maxim of the healthy groups, whose Oedipus is well. For a lasting and effective organization, it is enough to be ready to die for your ideas.

Theory of the Young Girl

At a structural (or "archetypal") level of analysis, the phallic function of the psyche is therefore the organizational capacity to unify a multitude, the anti-individualism par excellence. On the other hand, to disorganize is synonymous with individualizing, depoliticizing, losing the sense of the collective, breaking solidarity and cohesion, and pushing people to "play alone. Managing negatively to disorganize an enemy group therefore supposes to make it enter into a process that Lacan calls "phallic not-all". It is a critical process where the transcendent authority ensuring the cohesion of the group will be contested in the name of the oppression that it puts on the rights of the individuals to enjoy individually. Now it happens that this demand for individual enjoyment and this contestation of the authority of the Father are the typical behaviors suggested and required by the market and consumption.

For the Tiqqun collective (ancestor of the Invisible Committee), the figure of the bimbo, the sexy and desirable young girl, is the new authority figure of capitalism, the incarnation par excellence of this consumerist depoliticization. Figure of the disorganized individual, of the pure individual, one could say, the Young Girl is entropy personified, the very image of the death drive. One would be entitled to ask, however, why the depoliticized human is qualified here as "young" and "girl"? Isn't there an anti-youth racism and a misogyny at the origin of this? Tiqqun responds to these criticisms by placing things at an archetypal and symbolic level of analysis: "Let's understand: the concept of Young-Girl is obviously not a gendered concept. The nightclub lascar does not conform to it any less than the damsel dressed as a porn star. [...] In reality, the young girl is only the model citizen as redefined by the commercial society after the First World War, in explicit response to the revolutionary threat. [...] From now on, commodity society will look for its best supporters among the marginalized elements of traditional society - women and young people first, then homosexuals and immigrants. [...] "Young people and their mothers," Stuart Ewen acknowledges, "provided the way of life offered by advertising with the social principles of the consumer ethic. Young men because adolescence is the "period of life defined by a relationship of pure consumption to civil society." [Women because it is indeed the sphere of reproduction, over which they still reigned, that it was then about colonizing. Youth and Femininity hypostasized, abstracted and recoded into Youthfulness and Femininity will find themselves elevated to the rank of regulating ideals of imperial-citizen integration."[37]

To depoliticize and disorganize are thus strictly synonymous of making enter the consumption and the Spectacle. In other words, to disorganize a group, it is enough to "youth-fill" it, that is to say to contaminate its system of values by caricatural images of Youth and Femininity. Beyond its economic function, the world of advertising, where these images are widely disseminated, also plays a role of incapacitating social control. First of all, how does Femininity proceed? From the structural point of view, the women are subjects who, by definition, are not phallic, who certainly enjoy partially as the men, that is to say who also find sense in the life in community, but who, to be women, therefore different from the men, reserve themselves the right to be outlaw, subversive, not to enter the game of the social constraints and thus to refuse the structured organization of the groups, organization always perceived as masculine, even phallocrate or machist, therefore repressive and bad, refusal of the policy which leads them to look for sense in the sphere of the intimate, the eroticism and the fusional. Quest eternally doomed to failure, the sense arriving only in the social and the distinction. Julia Kristeva, psychoanalyst and feminist theorist, makes these deep reflections in a work dedicated to the new social pathologies (*borderlines*) appeared after the "sexual revolution" of the years 1960: "More radical, the feminist currents refuse the existing power and make of the second sex a counter-society. A feminine society is constituted, kind of alter ego of the official society, in which take refuge the hopes of pleasure. Against the sacrificial and frustrating sociosymbolic contract: the imagined harmonious counter-society,

---

37. TIQQUN, *Premiers matériaux pour une théorie de la Jeune-Fille*, Mille et une nuits, 2001, p. 10-12.

Governing by chaos

without prohibitions, free and enjoying. In our modern societies without beyond, the counter-society remains the only refuge of the enjoyment because it is precisely an atopia, place subtracted to the law, lock of the utopia.[38] The women always preserve an individualistic quant-à-soi with respect to the group and its organization. To press on this propensity to the individualistic enjoyment or, in other words, to persuade a group to adopt more feminine values, directed towards the intimate and the sexuality, allows to depoliticize a group and to make its organization impossible, therefore to make disappear its ideas in more or less long term, as well as its possible danger. The political police thus come to lodge themselves in places where one would not expect them, notably in the feminine press of all ages.

Then, how to disorganize by the Jeunitude? The cult of youth puts us on the slope of infantilization and of a pre-oedipal regression towards the primary processes of the psyche, that is to say the short-term, immature processes marked by the emotional, the irrational and the "magical thinking", on which *tittytainment* and *storytelling* are based. More widely, to disorganize and depoliticize a group and make it harmless, it is enough to attack its Oedipus. The Oedipus complex is the moment when the primordial mental structure at the foundation of all socialized and organized human life is internalized: it is the moment when the mental capacity to represent an organization chart, an articulated system of differentiated places, comes about. In a word, the aptitude to the dialectic and to the politics. The proto-organigram, which serves as matrix to all the others, is the psychocultural system of distinction AND of cooperative articulation between the places of men and women, and on the other hand of parents and children (by extension, of young and old). To attack the

---

38. Kʀɪsᴛᴇᴠᴀ (Julia), *Les nouvelles maladies de l'âme*, Fayard, 1993, p. 319.

Oedipus of a group, to attack its system of primordial distinctions between genders (men/women) and between generations (parents/children), is to attack its entire faculty of constituting an organizational chart, thus tipping it into organizational impotence and reducing it to juxtaposed individuals, incapable of communicating and cooperating. To promote the indistinction of roles and the exchange of places, as recommended by the theory of gender and fluid identities, in other words to put personal desire before respect for the group's organizational chart, all this facilitates the expression of phallic not-at-all individualism and is therefore a matter of strategies of disorganization. On a concrete behavioral level, this translates into a culture of the spontaneous, the impulsive, the visceral, the versatile and the search for immediate results, leading to an inability to concentrate, to plan and to develop long-term strategies.

The Young-Girl, that is to say the hysteria in power, culminates today in the LGBT and the figure of the transsexual and the *drag queen*, "new" new authoritarian figure of the unleashed and all-powerful libertarian liberalism. After decades of negative management, the phallic not-all and the de-œdipianized individualism are about to become dominant in the popular classes (petty bourgeoisie, middle classes, proletariat), where they already provoke all these pathological societal tendencies of devaluation of virility, over-valorization of femininity, hyperactive child-king and contempt for the elders, inducing in the end a total organizational impotence. The economically superior social strata also suffer from these mental viruses, but money is a powerful factor of social link (inter-gender and inter-generational), which allows them to keep a relative coherence. The fact remains that beyond the beautiful appearance, their background is just as dilapidated. And so all the social classes of the developed countries can intone in unison the maxim of the individualistic

Young-Girl and the model citizen of depoliticized groups: "No cause is worth fighting to the death for, my personal life comes before that of the group."

Biopower

Our overview of the multiple faces of contemporary scientific social control would be incomplete without a point on the Foucaultian notion of biopower. Indeed, it seems to us that beyond the power over minds, it is indeed a direct control of life, in the strictly biological sense of the term, that is sought by social engineering, whose ethos is affirmed as the incapacity to live and let live without intervening on the natural course of things. This interventionism, which can go as far as hacking, expresses, certainly, a spontaneous tendency of the human spirit to "epistemological voyeurism" and to the curiosity to understand everything that still escapes us, but it also translates a political project, the one carried by globalism, and whose conse-quences for life, in the biological sense of the term, will be worse than the totalitarianisms of the past centuries all together. Globalist social engineering is indeed placed under the sign of the *Great Reset,* but also of the *Gestell,* a concept worked on by Heidegger, qualifying the essence of what makes technological civilization and which Alain Finkielkraut, on the occasion of a debate with Peter Sloterdijk, Peter Weibel and Michel Houellebecq, tries to define as follows: "We had a lot of trouble translating it into French. It is translated as 'arrest', 'summons', 'putting at disposal'. It is quite simply the fact of the possibility of doing everything with everything. The possibility to make reality enter into an endless combinatorial. It seems to me that this is really what it is about at a moment, precisely, when this possibility does not concern only the inanimate matter, but also the living matter. It is the deepest tendency of modernity."[39]

This availability of everything for everything also means plasticity, flexibility, the possibility of completely rewriting the natural given, and thus total control over this natural given, mineral, vegetable or animal, environmental or subjective. Baudrillard, as for him, spoke about "perfect crime" to evoke this integral technological squaring of the real, this exterminating mesh consisting in not leaving the least atom untouched, and substituting to the lived world its reworked, retouched, smoothed, replaced version, in short, its simulacrum. The *Gestell*, or the scientific rationalization of the living, in other words the complete technological framing of the living and its chosification, is the guiding idea of the Great Transhumanist Reinitialization. As soon as the living can be completely quantified, digitized, explicated, reified, it can become the object of a serial management, an industrial production intrinsically docile to power, because it can be programmed and conditioned from the beginning. Social engineering thus culminates in genetic engineering (the hacking of DNA), eugenics, cloning, chimeras, these hybrid crossings of human and animal genetic material that the new bioethics laws want to make commonplace, the transfer of life into cyberspace (renamed "metaverse") and ultimately the legal replacement of humans by machines by granting robots the rights and legal personality of sentient beings, so as to erase the difference between living and non-living in the law (see the work of Anthony Bem and Alain Bensoussan, lawyers at the Paris Bar). All these researches find their

---

39. "The new conception of man. La construction de l'être humain", debate organized on May 3, 2000 by the Zentrum für Kunst und Medientechnologie (ZKM) and the Centre culturel français de Karlsruhe, in *Le Philosophoire* no. 23, autumn 2004: http://www.cairn.info/revue-le-philosophoire-2004-2-page-32.htm

Governing by chaos

best supporters in the promoters of transhumanism (Timothy Leary, Ray Kurzweil, Laurent Alexandre, Yuval Harari, etc.), an ideology coming from the counter-culture and the *New Age*, two currents themselves born from modern social control as Lutz Dammbeck shows in his documentary *Das Netz* ("The Web"), devoted to the history of cybernetics. The transformation of the human species is being taken care of at the highest level of the state in some countries. On September 12, 2022, Joe Biden, President of the United States, signed an Executive Order on Biotechnology and Biomanufacturing Innovation for a "Sustainable, Safe, and Secure U.S. Bioeconomy," from which we offer three translated excerpts below: "It is the policy of my Administration to coordinate a whole-of-government approach to advance biotechnology and biomanufacturing toward innovative solutions for health, climate change, energy, food security, agriculture, supply chain resilience, and national and economic security. [...] For biotechnology and biomanufacturing to help us achieve our societal goals, the United States must invest in fundamental scientific capabilities. We must develop genetic engineering technologies and techniques so that we can write circuits for cells and predictably program biology in the same way we write software and program computers; unleash the power of biological data, including through computational tools and artificial intelligence; and advance the science of large-scale production while reducing barriers to commercialization so that innovative technologies and products can reach markets more quickly. [...] The term "key areas of Research & Development" includes fundamental R&D of emerging biotechnologies, including biological engineering; predictive engineering of complex biological systems, including the design, construction, testing, and modeling of whole living cells, cellular components, or cellular systems; multidisciplinary quantitative and theoretical research to maximize convergence with other enabling technologies; and regulatory science, including the development of new information, criteria, tools, models, and approaches to inform and facilitate regulatory decision-making. These R&D priorities should be coupled with advances in predictive modeling, data analytics, artificial intelligence, bioinformatics, high-performance computing and other advanced information systems, data-driven metrics and standards, and other non-life science enabling technologies."[40]

The USA is the main driving force of biopower, because this country wants to remain at the head of the international competition. The advent of transhumanism is not the result of a conspiracy, but of techno-scientific power relations, i.e. decentralized and competitive interactions. As far as the human species is concerned, the technical development of tools and prostheses called weapons allows the natural capacities of the human body to be increased in order to prevail in the power relations. The whole world is therefore subject to technoscience, which overdetermines politics and geopolitics, i.e. the balance of power at the global level. For example, if Russia or China are able to ensure their political and geopolitical sovereignty in the face of NATO, it is because they have the weapons that make this possible, i.e. they have the techno-scientific development that makes this possible. It is the research and development of weapons - the arms race - that writes history, according to the competitive and conflictual mechanisms of game theory. The goal for each actor in the situation is to avoid the "capability gap" in the military vocabulary, i.e. to be technically surpassed by the enemy, and thus invaded and

---

40. "Executive Order on Advancing Biotechnology and Biomanufacturing Innovation for a Sustainable, Safe, and Secure American Bioeconomy," *White House*, September 12, 2022: https://www.whitehouse.gov/briefing-room/presidential-actions/2022/09/12/executive-order-on-advancing-biotechnology-and-biomanufacturing-innovation-for-a-sustainable-safe-and-secure-american-bioeconomy/

conquered by him one day or another. In 2023, we will not fight against NATO with bows and arrows. To fight with equal weapons, one must fight with equal technology, and therefore with equal technological risk, including in the anthropological field. The military-industrial complex of Russia or China is therefore forced to play the game of techno-scientific development to the full, with its civilian spin-offs and transhumanist drifts, which may in turn represent a threat to the political and geopolitical sovereignty of Russia and China. For example, from the point of view of economic warfare, to give up one's own digital currency is to submit to the digital currency of others. The competitive development of digital currencies is therefore inevitable and risks leading to the disappearance of material currencies, and therefore of private life. The augmentation of the human body by technology can also represent a diminution. According to Bernard Stiegler, the risk of getting lost in the dosage of the techno-scientific *pharmakon* is the Promethean abyss that specifically concerns the human species. We are all there. In other words - and Baudelaire would not deny it - everyone, you too, "hypocritical reader, my fellow man, my brother", is compromised to varying degrees in the *Great Reset*, since we are all beneficiaries of technoscience and we all use it intensively. And the only Homo sapiens who are not accomplices are gathered in a few Amazonian tribes without any sovereignty over their destiny, and whose future is entirely subject to the goodwill of people infinitely more powerful than them. These people do not live in the woods, but are agglomerating in sprawling metropolises, on their way to becoming *smart cities*, these so-called intelligent cities, entirely automated and which will no longer need humans to function. The replacement of supermarket cashiers by automatic tellers, supported by the marketing concept of directed self-production, is the prelude to the Great Replacement of the human by the robot.

To do with technoscience is therefore to take the risk of disappearing, but to do without technoscience is to disappear for sure. In order not to fall into a sterile technophobia, without falling into a self-destructive technophilia, let us affirm the absolute necessity to launch an international reflection on the articulation of life and technology, in the wake of the notions of archaeofuturism, or archaeomodernism, proposed by Guillaume Faye and Alexandre Douguine. As it subsists in its natural state, life poses a problem to power, because there is always something in it that escapes control. Nature is proliferation. Nature is free and decentralized. In contrast, capitalism is paid and centralized. Capitalism, however, is only a part of a whole, the paradigmatic opposition between right and left in politics becoming obsolete when we understand that power applies as a method social engineering and cybernetics, that is to say the commodification of the living. The historical process of transformation of subjects into objects obeys an anthropological and supra-political determinism. The Great Reinitialization, biopower, transhumanism and the *Gestell* all aim at the integral rewriting of reality in order to provide a better controlled, idealized, perfected version of it, and are therefore not only the horizon of practically all political powers since the advent of mass societies (Mesopotamia, Pharaonic Egypt), but also the guiding thread of all the great utopians, who have always spontaneously placed themselves at the service of the Prince. From Plato to the transhumanists, through Norbert Wiener, they have all tried to reduce existence to a gigantic *SimCity*, a vast automated process, univocal, from which contradiction and uncertainty have been removed. Obviously, it never works, for one simple reason: we are "still" alive.

Indeed, what hinders the integral control and the total reduction of uncertainty is the border between an interior and an exterior. In living beings, the skin, the epidermis, is this first border. The existence of an epidermal border ensuring the interface between an interiority and an exteriority is exactly what constitutes the irreducible specificity of all the living beings without exception and what distinguishes them from the non-living. There is life in the biological sense from the moment when there is epidermis, that is to say perception of a distinction between an interiority - the integrity of the creature -, and an exteriority - the environment. This integrity of the biological being makes it difficult to control it completely, or else with pathological after-effects and therefore a destruction of the system in the long run. It is on this basis that we can distinguish between non-living and living systems: non-living systems malfunction when they are not totally under control; conversely, living systems malfunction when they are totally under control. It is this generalized dysfunction leading to a collapse of human societies into the idiocracy that awaits post-humanity from the laboratories. The general question that biopower, identified with contemporary political power, asks itself is the following: what are we going to do with biomass? What are we going to do with the living? Any living being with a self-preservation instinct and a will to power necessarily asks this question, but contemporary biopower hopes to provide a final solution. In his various interventions, Yuval Harari announces the end of natural selection and its replacement by a purely cultural selection carried out by science. In other words, the end of a decentralized and unconscious process of emergence of life by adaptation to its environment, and its replacement by a controlled process of invention of new forms of life according to a conscious planning (*intelligent design*). Harari thus announces, without even realizing it, the end of what works and its replacement by what does not work, or only with crutches. Natural selection is the mechanism by which living things adapt to the environment as it is, or disappear. Its process is in essence rewarding in its effort, it can only tolerate what works. What does not work disappears, or remains marginal, a minority. On the contrary, the cultural project, always a conscious project, has always also a dimension of Promethean insurrection against the environment as it is. The cultural project is a forcing of the real, it wants to bend the environment to its will, it wants to bend the territory to the map. A scientifically created form of life would not appear on Earth according to the same modalities as the other living beings, by instinctive adaptation, but by conscious imitation, biomimicry, such as a copy which would come to compete with the original on its ground. Genetic engineering makes appear Golems and Frankenstein's monsters, artificial beings conceived consciously, thus condemned to imitate life, but in less good, in less adapted. Will the Promethean dialectic between nature and culture end in a Pyrrhic victory for culture? The replacement of nature by culture would in fact be a replacement of the living by parodic artifacts, opening the way to the advent of the pseudo-living. Let us explain.

The more we go up in the evolution, and the more the interiority of the living is strong, until leading to the possibility of making real hiding towards the outside. It is what we call mental, psychological intimacy, etc., and which allows to go until the lie. This possibility proper to the living to hide things to the external glance is unbearable for the power, which sees it a form of resistance to its inquisitive exercise. This impossibility of total control comes from the fact that no one has a total right to look at the creature, no one is able to have an integral access to the interiority, from where this relative unpredictability of the biological, whose traceability is never guaranteed. The abolition of the biological, that is to say of the very principle of all borders and limits, or at least the complete framing of the biological by the digital, should allow the abolition of this uncertainty, the integral access to the interiority, thus the complete transgression of the integrity of the creature, the possibility of ending all forms of secrecy and thus the total control of all forms of conscious life. Internet is an extraordinary source of information, but it is also a space of total transparency. Internal" creatures would be in its image. In fact, a digital consciousness would only be a simulated form of life since it would be without epidermis, or a simulated epidermis, therefore false. Indeed, the programmer has a total right of control over his program, he can rectify it as he wants and reduce totally the uncertainty of its functioning. The programmer is in a "divine" position. There can therefore be no digital life since the minimum required, the real uncertainty linked to the real epidermis, is not present. By definition, true uncertainty is neither modelable nor programmable. On the other hand, there can be extermination of the biological in favor of a form of "simulated life" in the digital. Realization of the "perfect crime", the extermination of the uncertainty linked to the true real - here, the living matter - for the benefit of a simulation of the real perfectly traceable and controlled.

The pouring of our lives into the virtual Matrix and the access of the Power to the psychological intimacy of the citizens are nevertheless advancing in great steps, notably thanks to the ever more precise software of analysis of the emotional reactions elaborated in artificial intelligence. We are already partially downloaded in the cyberspace and the metaverse, considering the time we spend on the Internet and the increasing dependence in which we are towards it. This tendency is obviously supported by the power, as we can see by reading the recommendations of the digital lobby. As early as 2004, the Groupement des Industries de l'Interconnexion des Composants et des Sous-Essemblées Electroniques (GIXEL) - of which Pierre Gattaz was president before becoming the president of the MEDEF - made the following recommendations in its little Blue Book: "The transition from physical identity to digital identity is becoming more and more important in all environments because of the development of ICTs, and in particular the Internet. [Acceptance by the population: In our democratic societies, security is very often seen as an infringement of individual freedoms. It is therefore necessary to make the population accept the technologies used, including biometrics, video surveillance and controls. Several methods will have to be developed by public authorities and industrialists to make biometrics accepted. They will have to be accompanied by an effort of user-friendliness through recognition of the person and by the provision of attractive functionalities: - Education from kindergarten onwards, children will use this technology to enter the school, leave the school, have lunch at the canteen, and parents or their representatives will identify themselves to pick up the children. - Introduction in consumer goods, comfort or games: cell phone, computer, car, home automation, video games. - Develop "cardless" services at the bank, in the supermarket, in transport, for Internet access... The same approach cannot be taken to make surveillance and control technologies accepted, it will probably be necessary to resort to persuasion and regulation by demonstrating the contribution of these technologies to the serenity of the populations and by minimizing the inconvenience [*sic*] caused. Here again, electronics and computer science can make a significant contribution to this task." [41]

The greatest genocide in history, that of the entire biosphere, has already begun. In *Comment les riches détruisent la planète*, Hervé Kempf describes the major lines of this globalist *Gestell* at the ecological and political levels. On a strictly geopolitical level, it consists in playing with the lives of millions, even billions of human beings.

---

41. GIXEL, *Blue Book. Grands programmes structurants. Proposals from the electronic and digital industries*, 2004, p. 5 and 35: http://www.gfie.fr/fr/images_db/Livre%20bleu.pdf

This geopolitical game takes two forms: the free recombination of borders, on the one hand, and demographic control, on the other. As we have seen, the abolition of borders is the reign of death, both on a biological and psychic level. There is no psychic life, that is to say production of meaning, except in the uncertainty and the confrontation with something that resists, with a real of some kind, a border, a limit. If the borders no longer resist, it is the very principles of identity, distinction and semantic elaboration that waver, signalling in the long run the collapse of the system on itself, or else its survival in a liminal space that is that of the "zombie", halfway between life and death. The geopolitical *Gestell*, the voluntarist recomposition of borders, as in Europe with the creation of euroregions that obey only commercial logics, is therefore a kind of hallucinated mysticism of generalized crossbreeding, such as that defended in his time by Richard de Coudenhove-Kalergi (1894-1972), one of the founding fathers of the European Union, an expression of this general process of de-œdipianization whose guiding fantasy seems to be the creation of a totally plastic and flexible form of life, in a word the ideal slave, whose identity has no more ties, no more origins, and can therefore be rewritten at will.

Only a drastic demographic control will allow the development of this zombified future humanity. In the continuity of the theories of Thomas Malthus (1766-1834), various demographic reduction programs have been implemented with varying degrees of success in various countries over the last two centuries. In 2010, *Le Monde* mentioned the eugenicist and anti-natalist cogitations carried out at the UN to reduce the population under ecological pretexts and added: "Almost at the same time, a report, elaborated by the London School of Economics (LSE) at the request of the Optimum Population Trust (OPT) - a British NGO militating for the reduction of the world's population - estimated that the least costly way of solving the problem of global warming would be to reduce the world's population by 500 million individuals by 2050. But since most projections call for the total population to rise to more than 9 billion by then, the proposal to reduce the world's population to just 6 billion implies eliminating 3 billion people..."[42]

All means are good to achieve depopulation, whether by preventing births or, when beings are born, by premeditated mass murder. The role of the various supranational bodies, NGOs or others, lies above all in the planning of crises, wars, epidemics and famines, notably by means of the Codex Alimentarius. From a general point of view, biopower consists in governing by maintaining a threat to the physical survival of populations, a threat that does not have to be real to be effective. The Iron Mountain report, published in the 1960s under the direction of the economist John Galbraith and entitled *Unwanted Peace? A Report on the Utility of Wars*, is perfectly clear on this subject: "The existence of an external threat to which credence is given is, therefore, essential to social cohesion as well as to the acceptance of political authority. The threat must be plausible, its magnitude must be commensurate with the complexity of the threatened society, and it must appear, at the very least, to weigh on the whole of society."[43] Defining an enemy, a founding gesture of politics according to Carl Schmitt. But who said that the enemy had to be real?

42. "Should the world population be reduced to save the planet?", *Le Monde*, January 18, 2010: https://www.lemonde.fr/planete/article/2010/01/18/faut-il-reduire-la-popu-lation-mondiale-pour-sauver-la-planete_5976998_3244.html
43. GALBRAITH (John), *The Unwanted Peace? A Report on the Utility of Wars*, Calmann-Lévy, 1968, p. 113.

Provisional conclusion
How to defeat the utopia of the *Great Reset*?

Having summarized its past, let's ask ourselves what is the future of social engineering. It is the Great Narrative to pass the Great Reinitialization, that is to say the imposition of a transhumanist dictatorship putting an end to the human species, but preserving the appearances of democratic debate and diversity of opinions. To achieve this in a society of communication and transparency, the power can no longer be satisfied with lying shamelessly, it must learn to "deceive without lying. Propaganda is renamed "public relations" or "influence" and becomes grey propaganda, a mixture of true and false to better convey the false. Since authoritarianism and total dissimulation are difficult to maintain in the long term, the authorities apply, for example, the *Nudges* method, the progression by stages and by small inciting and non compelling touches, and the principle of the pretext, consisting in making pass something under the cover of something else. In this case, to pass a computer dictatorship of the Chinese "social credit" type under the pretext of treating people or saving the planet.

The defeat of this totalitarian project depends on the ability to answer practical questions. In wartime, the most important questions are methodological. Military art is an art of execution, with its two strategic and tactical aspects, the long term and the short term.

Theoretical, ideological and ethical questions must be reserved for times of peace. When one is already engaged in conflict, everything must be subordinated to a single priority: how to win the balance of power? The enemy today considers that all blows are permitted. All blows are allowed means that cunning is allowed to camouflage that all blows are allowed. This is why the enemy advances behind a bureaucratic and technocratic institutional screen that gives it an appearance of legitimacy and legality. In our Kafkaesque world, that is where the power lies. It is therefore necessary to place oneself at this level as well and not to hesitate to use cunning to support the balance of power on equal terms in this institutional field. Power lies to us, so we must lie to power, but hide the lie. We are at war, we must change the paradigm compared to times of peace: the objective of politics is not to respect values, but to win a balance of power. To win at all costs, because it is absurd to believe that one can respect values if one is dead. To parody Charles Péguy on Kantian morality: "Virtue has beautiful hands, but it has no hands".

No morality, no ethics must inhibit us to win the balance of power. We must be beyond Good and Evil, to use the Nietzschean formula. How can we do this? We must measure our action by its concrete and practical value in suppressing the enemy, and that is all. To achieve this, the precise definition of who the enemy is is secondary. Why is this so? Because one may well have identified who the enemy is, or who the enemies are, for there are always several, but be mistaken about the nature of the battlefield. It is a diversionary strategy of the enemy to mislead us on a false battlefield, which will lead us to shoot in the void, even if we have understood who the enemy is. On the other hand, if we define the battlefield precisely, all the shots will hit, directly or indirectly, because the environment is appropriate, the context is right, the framing is right. We will fire in the right direction, even if we do not see clearly who the enemy is. The enemy uses institutions, bureaucracy, and technocracy as a battlefield to camouflage himself, so that's where we need to respond. And to further optimize the practical value of the question, it can be rephrased as: "What can I concretely do to defeat the *Great Reset* on the battlefield of institutions?" If I overestimate my strengths and give myself goals that are beyond what I can concretely do, I too am in utopia. We don't do what we want, we do what we can. To this question, it is up to each person to answer according to his or her concrete means.

The centralized power that is trying to be established at the global level has no democratic legitimacy. The European Union is the most striking illustration of this. An enlightened despotism, genuinely concerned with the interests of the people, would be tolerable at the limit, but we are already far from it. In this case, the risk of extinction that the Great Reinitialization poses, not only to humanity, but to all forms of intelligence, is the most serious that history has ever known. In fact, its project is indeed to complete History. For it is not this or that human group that the globalist Reinitialization seeks to exterminate, but the species in its entirety, and even beyond that, the simple capacity for intelligible articulation of a signifying discourse. Faced with this unheard-of violence, resistance must be organized. However, if we want it to be constructive and not stagnate in incoherent and acephalous riots or sterile terrorism, this resistance must imperatively be organized, planned, calculated, strategic, with a view to an institutional seizure of power, essentially by the slow infiltration of the structures of power. Protest remains harmless as long as it remains visible, outside the system or in the street. It must be replaced by an invisible subversion, situated at the heart of the system and inscribed in the long term. The coming insurrection must be conceived, thought out, methodical and rational. The propaedeutic to any overthrow of illegitimate power therefore needs a military type of organization, and not only a militant one, nourished by a deep tactical and strategic reflection, itself supported by an education in the culture of intelligence, espionage and counter-espionage, as well as by a systematic profiling and listing of those who profile us and list us. Knowing our enemy, applying to him what he applies to us, re-establishing the equality of the couple "seeing and being seen", in short, hacking the pirates to answer the question that Juvenal asked himself: "Who will keep the guards?

A model of organization was proposed to us by History: it is the National Council of the Resistance (CNR), formed following the call launched by a certain colonel de Gaulle in exile, and which gathered women and men of all political, social, and religious origins, to fight against the Nazi invader. Today, the enemy of mankind has changed. He is no longer identifiable with a particular geopolitical zone. He belongs to this "transnational class of privileged people" of which Jacques Attali speaks, an economically dominant oligarchy, which is actively working on the systemic architecture of globalization according to the engineering methods we have described, and which Warren Buffett claims is winning the war against the working classes. The war has thus been declared. In response, we want to use this text to make our contribution to a future Second National Council of the Resistance. Our manifesto, reproduced below, will be the call of the Veterans of the CNR launched in 2004 to commemorate the 60th anniversary of the program of the National Council of the Resistance, a political program conceived by the people, for the people, and which the oligarchy said had to be methodically deconstructed. By laying this first stone, our goal is to federate in a sacred Union all the wills to fight against the common enemy, which today takes the face of this New World Order founded on the strategy of shock, planned chaos, programmed economic or sanitary crises, the virtualization of Meaning and the brandishing of a terrorist, or sanitary, or climatic threat, as you wish, to justify the concentrationary surveillance of populations.

If this system doesn't collapse on its own, then we'll have to help it do so. We will do it. There are many of us. There are millions of us. Millions of times more than our enemy. He is afraid of us. He trembles with terror, because he knows that his power is fragile and rests only on the bluff and the credit we give him. All his strength is based on representations that we have believed. Let's stop believing, let's stop obeying and the reality will appear: we are stronger than him. The king is naked. Moreover, his own power makes him suffer, because he knows deep down that it is based on lies. Unconsciously, he asks us to hit him to bring him back to his senses. Let's not deprive ourselves. He will thank us in the end.

The Call of the Resistants

Call for the commemoration of the 60th anniversary of the program of the National Council of the Resistance of March 15, 1944.

At a time when we see the foundation of the social achievements of the Liberation being called into question, we, veterans of the Resistance movements and the fighting forces of Free France (1940-1945), call on the younger generations to keep alive and pass on the heritage of the Resistance and its ever-present ideals of economic, social and cultural democracy.

Sixty years later, Nazism is defeated, thanks to the sacrifice of our brothers and sisters in the Resistance and the nations united against fascist barbarism. But the threat has not completely disappeared and our anger against injustice is still intact.

We call, in conscience, to celebrate the actuality of the Resistance, not for the benefit of partisan causes or instrumentalized by any power issue, but to propose to the generations that will succeed us to accomplish three humanistic and profoundly political gestures in the true sense of the word, so that the flame of the Resistance will never go out:

We call first of all on educators, social movements, public communities, creators, citizens, the exploited, the humiliated, to celebrate together the anniversary of the program of the National Council of the Resistance (CNR) adopted in clandestinity on March 15, 1944: social security and generalized pensions, control of the "economic feudalities", the right to culture and education for all, a press freed from money and corruption, social laws for workers and farmers, etc. How can there be a lack of money today to maintain and extend these social conquests, when the production of wealth has increased considerably since the Liberation, a period when Europe was ruined? The political, economic and intellectual leaders and the whole of society must not resign or allow themselves to be impressed by the current international dictatorship of the financial markets which threatens peace and democracy.

We then call upon the movements, parties, associations, institutions and unions that are heirs to the Resistance to go beyond sectoral issues, and to devote themselves first and foremost to the political causes of injustices and social conflicts, and not only to their consequences, to define together a new "program of Resistance" for our century, knowing that fascism always feeds on racism, intolerance and war, which themselves feed on social injustices.

Finally, we call upon children, young people, parents, elders and grandparents, educators, public authorities, to a true peaceful insurrection against the mass media which propose as a horizon for our youth only commercial consumption, contempt for the weakest and for culture, generalized amnesia, and the excessive competition of all against all. We do not accept that the main media are from now on controlled by private interests, contrary to the program of the National Council of the Resistance and the ordinances on the press of 1944.

More than ever, to those who will make the century that is beginning, we want to say with our affection: "To create is to resist. To resist is to create."

Signatories: Lucie Aubrac, Raymond Aubrac, Henri Bartoli, Daniel Cordier, Philippe Dechartre, Georges Guingouin, Stéphane Hessel, Maurice Kriegel-Valrimont, Lise London, Georges Séguy, Germaine Tillion, Jean-Pierre Vernant, Maurice Voutey.

Sunday, March 14, 2004

Best sellers Max Milo Editions

Hitler's banker, Jean-François Bouchard

Confessions of a forger, Éric Piedoie Le Tiec

The Koran and the flesh, Ludovic-Mohamed Zahed

Governing by fake news, Jacques Baud

Governing by chaos, Collectif

A political history of food, Paul Ariès

Mad in U.S.A.: The ravages of the "American model",
Michel Desmurget

Mondial soccer club geopolitics, Kévin Veyssière

Putin: Game master?, Jacques Braud

Treatise on the three impostors: Moses, Jesus, Muhammad,
The Spirit of Spinoza

TV Lobotomy, Michel Desmurget